About the Author

Alasdair White is a consultant specialising
in human resource management and
organisational development, with over
10 years' experience in senior management
and board level consultancy. Working for
Performance Management Solutions Ltd, he
is based in Brussels and has an international
practice with clients throughout Britain,
Europe, the Middle East, Africa and the Far
East. He is an external tutor on the MBA
programme at Henley Management College
in the UK and a visiting speaker at
Management Centre Europe in Belgium
and also at the IBM European Training
Centre at La Hulpe, Belgium. He is the
author of *Managing for Performance* and
Continuous Quality Improvement, both
published by Piatkus.

G000140486

ALASDAIR WHITE

THE ESSENTIAL GUIDE TO

DEVELOPING YOUR STAFF

HOW TO RECRUIT, TRAIN, COACH AND MENTOR TOP-QUALITY PEOPLE

PIATKUS

Copyright © 1998 by PMS Limited

First published in 1998 by
Judy Piatkus (Publishers) Ltd of
5 Windmill Street, London W1P 1HF

This paperback edition published in 1999

The author has asserted his moral rights

*A catalogue record for this book is available
from the British Library*

ISBN 0–7499–1722–9 (hbk)
     0–7499–1889–6 (pbk)

Text design: Suzanne Perkins/Grafica

Set by Action Typesetting Ltd, Gloucester
Printed and bound in Great Britain by
Mackays of Chatham PLC, Chatham, Kent

To Fiona, Riba and Siobhan as always

Acknowledgements

My thanks go to all those who have contributed to the development and publication of this book. In particular, I would like to thank Adrian Kennedy for his inspiration; Gill Cormode of Piatkus for her continuing faith; Rachel Winning and her colleagues at Piatkus for their efforts in turning the manuscript into a book; and my wife, Fiona, for the sanity checks on what I wrote, her proof reading, her patience and her encouragement. As always, the actual words are mine and any errors and omissions are also mine.

Alasdair White
Belgium
1998

Contents

Introduction

As the market place becomes ever more discerning, companies are seeking new and different ways of giving themselves a competitive advantage. New products, new image and new marketing ideas are just some of the ways this can be achieved but the truly successful companies will focus on their people to provide the leading edge.

The days of treating staff as disposable resources are long over and to be a genuinely market-leading company you must develop your staff to provide a long-lasting competitive advantage. This requires you to get the right people in the right jobs, to train and coach them and then to adopt practices that will enable them to maintain their

THE FIVE KEYS TO DEVELOPING TOP-QUALITY PEOPLE

- **Recruitment** – Getting the right people in the right jobs

- **Developing People** – Training and coaching to ensure the right skills are used in the right way

- **Mentoring** – Using mentoring to ensure long-term development and performance

- **Developing Managers** – Ensuring these key people are delivering the leadership the organisation requires

- **Managing for Performance** – Techniques that ensure top-quality performance

performance and to deliver the benefits you are seeking. You will also need to provide leadership through the management structure.

In this book we will be looking at the five key areas that will ensure your staff deliver their full potential.

PART ONE: RECRUITMENT

Getting the right people in the right job

Staff are just too valuable and too expensive a resource to treat in a cavalier manner and we need to make sure we have the right people doing the right jobs.

In the following four chapters we will be looking at:

- Preparing the right job description

- Finding the right person for the job

- Recruiting the right person

- Getting them started in the right way

CHAPTER ONE

You want to recruit someone – but what do you want them to do?

So, you've decided you want to recruit someone. Perhaps you need to expand, a new role has been created or there is too much work for the current team and a new person seems the logical thing. Recruiting a new person to the team can be profoundly satisfying and profitable – it can also be a very expensive disaster. How profitable, or how disastrous, will be determined by how well you carry out the recruitment process.

The first step of this process is to define the job.

JOB DEFINITION CHECKLIST

1	Decide on how many people you really need
2	Prepare a Job Description and Specification
3	Establish the Job Title
4	Determine the Minimum Performance Standards
5	Determine the skills needed
6	Establish the reporting line
7	Establish the employment conditions and costs

---

1 How many people do you need? – A strategic issue

The correct allocation of resources – capital, cash flow, people – is decided by the long-term strategy of the business and not by the short-term tactics being used to deliver the company's objectives. The normal strategic approach will determine what the company will sell, how they will sell it, at what price, and in which markets. From this all the other strategic criteria can be developed. One such criterion is how many people and what skills are needed to deliver the objectives you have tasked the company with.

But there is an assumption, often made at this point, that can throw all the calculations – it is that all the people will work at 100% capacity for 100% of the time. And this is just plain wrong.

To illustrate this point, take a sales team and a management team – two groups often affected by the problem of capacity versus targets.

A sales team

Sales people can divide their activity into the following categories:

- Sales interviews with potential and existing clients

- Prospecting and setting up interviews

- Administration connected to sales interviews

- Administration connected with management

- Non-business related activity – coffee, toilet, gossip, etc.

To calculate capacity, allocate a realistic amount of time to each of these categories *based on what your people are currently doing* and it becomes obvious a large amount of a sales person's time is taken up with non-selling activity as illustrated by the last two categories above.

One sales team in a large company found that:
(1) Administration connected with management – covering weekly and monthly reports, compliance reports, activity sheets, attending meetings and responding to management memos and requests - accounted for 16 to 20 hours each month which is just short of one hour per working day.
(2) Non-business related activity – coffee, toilet, gossip, etc. – all of which was necessary, was taking up a further one hour per day.

Taking all this into account, the sales team were spending about two hours per day on non-sales activity: while this may sound reasonable, remember that two hours in each normal working day is equivalent to 25% of the working time. Thus, each sales person was doing their job (selling) for just 75% of the time.

A management team

A similar calculation can be done for management teams. Here, meetings seem to be the major issue. If a meeting involves more than one other person and more than one topic requiring discussion, then that meeting will take more than 30 minutes with the time taken being proportional to the number of people present wishing to speak on each topic. Most meetings seem to take between 60 and 90 minutes. Add 15 minutes for preparation and around 30 minutes for follow-up, and a meeting of 90 minutes will take over two hours. Add in the non-role-specific activity (management-imposed time and non-work activity) of around two hours per day and it is not surprising that a manager will be spending around 75% of his time either in meetings or non-productive activity.

The productivity gap

From a capacity point of view, it would be perfectly reasonable to assume that no one is working productively more than 75% of their time and many are working at less than 60%. If this is the case, and there is little reason to doubt it, then a member of any team is producing only a maximum of 3.75 man days of work per five-day week.

In a five-person team, for example, this gives a total productivity output of 18.75 days out of 25 – a productivity gap of 6.25 days.

At this point you may say: yes, but if we bring in an additional person we will address this issue. But, one extra person pushes the total available days up to 30 and the productive days up to 22.5. So, even bringing in an extra person will not address the original productivity gap and the real gap has expanded from 6.25 days lost to 7.5 days. And the costs have gone up by 20%. The problem is even worse, of course, if the actual productive time is, say, 60%.

Some companies address this problem by expecting their people to work long hours or to put in 'overtime'. This is understandable since it is designed to deal with the productivity gap – if people were more efficient in the use of their time then they wouldn't need to work long hours – but it is not acceptable as an alternative to recruitment. That many people accept this situation is as much a reflection of their approach to work as it is of the company culture.

Other areas of lost time

Even if you can get people to be productive for 75% of their time (a practical, rather than theoretical, maximum) there are still other areas of 'lost' time that must be taken into account – training, sick leave, and holidays being the principal ones. In Europe today, many people are entitled to 25 working days' holiday each year plus the public holidays –

since the average number of public holidays in Europe is 12 days per country, the total amount of 'lost' time is around 37 working days.

To this can be added approximately 5 sick days and 5 training days, giving a total of 47 working days 'lost' as far as productivity is concerned. As there are 260 weekdays available in a year this means that the average person works just 213 days or 82% of the available time. And at 75% capacity, the real productive time is 75% × 213 = 160 days or 61% of the weekdays in the year. Is it any wonder that goals based on 100% productivity for 100% of the time fail to be achieved?

This is not to suggest that you ban people from being sick, or that training should be cancelled, or that holiday entitlement be cut – but you need to keep in mind that a well-run and productive team is only productive 61% of the time and you need to adjust the goals accordingly.

The first thing you need to do is to check to see if the goals have been set correctly, based upon what your people are *actually* doing. Most companies set their goals based on some projected target that they wish to achieve – rather than on current performance – and you will need to be sure you understand how they do this and to consider the resources required.

Addressing the productivity gap

If the goals cannot be adjusted – and this is the case in any number of companies – then capacity needs to be increased through acquisition of new resources. But recruiting more people is a long-term investment and the overheads will rise – and if you find you have recruited beyond your resources, you can't just downsize at will without incurring additional restructuring costs (or facing unfair dismissal or redundancy payments). Could the capacity issue be handled by a one-off investment in technology – which will result in increased productivity? Could outsourcing some activities free up manpower for other, more productive, activities? Could you get higher performance by using performance management techniques? Could you ...?

A vicious circle

If you have done everything possible to improve perfor-mance and there is still a gap between what the current performance can deliver and the goals that have been set by the company, then the correct solution is to recruit more people. The question is: how many?

Consider, for a moment, a five-person team. If the team goals can only be delivered by each member delivering 100% for 100% of the time, then 25 days' work per week is required. However, at 61% effective productivity, each person is delivering only three days per week or a total of 15 days' work per week for the team. The shortfall is 10 days' work – and since you cannot assume that any recruit will produce more than the team average of 61%, you will need FOUR new members of staff – this would meet the goals with two days' spare to increase capacity.

Unfortunately, it also means the number and cost of staff has increased by 80% – which might not go down too well with cost-conscious senior management. But it is justifiable if it will provide an 80% increase in the productivity of the team.

So, even if the right solution is to recruit more people, you will still have to reassess the goals of the team – if you don't, or senior management won't, then the cycle of failure will inevitably repeat itself.

OK, so you DO need more people

You have done all the calculations and improvements and the solution is to recruit more people. You even know how many you need. But do you know what you *really* want them to do?

The 'bums on seats' approach is, in today's cost-conscious and responsible company, a total non-starter – or should be. We just cannot afford the investment in time and money to develop the wrong people. It would be far better to recruit the right people in the first place: they become productive far faster, they cost less in development terms, and they add value to the company.

If you are to get the right people into the right jobs then the first thing you need to do is to define exactly what the job entails and how it fits in with the rest of the company's activities.

2 The Job Description – A specification sheet

You have a specific job that needs doing – a job that requires the person to carry out particular tasks and to accept certain responsibilities. The person will need a range of attributes and skills and they will need to deliver a pre-defined minimum performance standard. The job interacts with other jobs in the company and has a specific reporting line.

You know all these things, but to keep the recruitment process focused you will need a job specification to ensure you pick the right person. A job specification is usually referred to as a Job Description but the idea of *specifications* is vital – it suggests that the 'specs' are the cold, hard requirements, the key to the job and not a woolly feel-good description. Specifications fall into one of three categories: prerequisites, 'nice to have', and those that are considered only if everything else is equal.

When you select a new computer you will be looking for some very specific functions. These are the functions that you consider prerequisites: perhaps a large-capacity hard disk, a floppy drive, a colour monitor, telecommunication capability, a CD-ROM drive, the ability to run certain types of program. If the computer does not have all of these, then you will reject it.

Then there are the functions that are of secondary importance: perhaps the overall speed of the micro-processor, interconnectivity with other types of computers and operating systems, the ability to have an internal or external modem, file and program sharing. These functions are 'nice to have' and will help in selecting the right machine.

Finally, there are those features that are of little significance to you: the colour of the equipment, the size of each piece, and the overall price — after all, most computers seem to be the same basic colour, size and price. These features are considered only if all the other factors are equal.

This is self-evident and you would be surprised if anyone based their decisions on whether it was the right colour, or fitted in with their decor. You would expect people to make the decision based on the specifications they wanted. The

JOB DESCRIPTION CONTENTS

1   Functional job title

2   Corporate job title

3   General description

4   Key responsibilities and Minimum Performance Standards

5   Secondary responsibilities and Minimum Performance Standards

6   Reporting line – up and down

7   Employment terms (including remuneration)

best match between the specifications and the functions offered will determine the equipment chosen.

And yet, when it comes to recruitment, decisions are often based on whether the candidate is a 'nice person' and would 'fit in' with the team rather than on whether they can do the job. The purpose of the Job Description is to keep the process focused on what is really important – the ability of the person to do what we want them to do.

3 Functional and corporate job titles

The functional job title

This explains what a person does in the organisation – secretary, lathe operator, manager, supervisor, draftsman, driver, store assistant. It must clearly encapsulate the main functions of the job. A person whose main responsibility is typing letters is a typist, not a secretary. However, if their main responsibilities are to run the office, maintain the diaries, act as receptionist, supervise others and do some typing, then secretary or office manager would be a better functional title.

The corporate job title

The corporate job title, on the other hand, has more to do with a person's status – the manager of the sales team may have the corporate title of Vice-President – Sales, the workshop manager may have the official title of Production Manager, a secretary may be called a Personal Assistant.

Corporate titles are often a very important status symbol both for the person and for the way that person's job is viewed. In some cultures – such as the US – the corporate job title is perceived as so important that you are unlikely to meet an American manager who is not the Vice-President of something or another. The right job title can also be very important for doing business in other countries – an impressive sounding title may well get you in to see the decision-maker more easily, and this is particularly true of places like Japan, Asia, South America, and the Middle East.

Corporate job titles are also a source of reward and recognition and many employees will strive to achieve a particular title. In one American bank the objective of almost all managers was to be a vice-president. That ALL managers above regional manager or department head were vice-presidents – and there were many thousands of them – did not seem to dim its attraction.

Within your company you will probably have a corporate title for each of the senior jobs. If this is the case then you will need to 'signal' the position of the new person by giving them a suitable title. For example: if you have a Marketing Director, the functional sales manager may need to be called the Sales Director if they are at the same level in the corporate structure. But a word of warning: there is something slightly ludicrous about a company of 20 people having a Sales Director in charge of a department of two.

General description

The 'general description' should cover all aspects of the job so that anyone reading it will have a good idea of what is involved. This description is for a 'senior secretary':

> The role of the secretary in the General Manager's office is to act as the first point of contact for anyone wishing to speak to the GM. This will require answering the telephone, taking accurate messages, opening all post, and acting as receptionist for all visitors. The secretary is also responsible for maintaining, but not controlling, the GM's business diary. Routine retrieval of data from the computer and hard-copy filing systems and the preparation of new data for filing is also a prime responsibility. The GM drafts all his own

correspondence on his computer but the secretary is responsible for the preparation of the final copy for signature and for filing. The GM's secretary is also responsible for assisting the other senior managers in handling their routine secretarial requirements.

There are, of course, many other activities that the General Manager's secretary will carry out during the day, but the general description would allow anyone to understand the primary function of the job.

The following example, on the other hand, shows how *not* to write a general description. It is for a software development manager in a large oil company.

This company prides itself on being at the leading edge of software development for all aspects of the upstream and exploration work. The role of the software development manager is to maintain that leading edge, to anticipate all problems and to move swiftly to address those problems if they arise. He will be working in a tight-knit and focused team to which he must make a positive contribution for the benefit of the company.

Yes, but what is the main job of this person? This sounds more like an advertisement than a general description. What exactly is a 'leading edge', what will be his relationship to the team, what is a 'positive contribution', and so on? Here is a possible re-write:

The software development manager is responsible for directing and supervising the work of a team of six programming specialists involved in developing and maintaining the software used by the company to interpret geological data, map oil reservoirs and control the product flow through all parts of the up-stream and

13

exploration functions. The primary responsibility of the development manager is to ensure that the software the team develops will enable the company to become more efficient in those areas to which the software relates and to maintain their market lead in all aspects of up-stream and exploration activity.

The writing of the general description can, and should, be revisited when the full job description is complete, but at this stage this first attempt will help you focus on what the job is about so that you can start writing down the responsibilities.

Key responsibilities – the main specifications

This requires considerable thought and you should take as much time as is necessary so that you can clearly establish exactly what responsibilities the person will have to undertake. After all, this is what the person is being recruited to do.

It is sometimes easier to approach this process by listing all the activities and responsibilities that are involved in the job and to make a selection of what is a primary responsibility, what is secondary and what would be a 'nice to have'.

The primary responsibilities are those that the person *must* fulfil to do the job. The secondary responsibilities are those they should *try to* fulfil. If the person has delivered all the primary responsibilities then they have done the job but if they have also delivered the secondary responsibilities they have exceeded the basic requirements and have delivered added value. The 'nice to have' elements should, at this stage, be ignored, as they are not important to the job.

Job responsibilities are not just a series of actions, they are also a performance standard and should be written as such. The format is 'One of the key responsibilities is to carry out an action in the following way or to the following standard' – a sort of 'what has to be done, to what level, by when' structure.

For example:

To file all letters

is a statement of responsibility but it is incomplete, whereas

To file all letters, according to the current filing system, each day so that no letter is left unfiled at the end of each working day

is a statement of responsibility and a definition of the minimum performance standard (MPS), the result of which is measurable or observable.

Equally:

To submit reports as and when required by management

is again incomplete and should be redefined as follows:

To submit monthly reports covering .... to the immediate supervisor by the fifth working day of the following month

and this, once again, defines the MPS for the action.

It is also very important to avoid the woolly statements so beloved of those who think they are being clever. For example:

To work hard at implementing the strategic plan to the benefit of the company as a whole

or

To encourage the team to work together in a productive manner so as to deliver the goals they have been tasked with

15

Both these are from a 'wish list' and have no place on a job description as they are open to interpretation and have not been defined in MPS terms.

The more senior the job, the more complex the job description and the longer the list of key responsibilities: but it is better to have twenty or more key responsibilities and a number of secondary responsibilities than to try to describe the job in a few lines. Remember, you are constructing the specification sheet for the job and it needs to be as detailed as possible.

4 Minimum Performance Standards

Minimum Performance Standards are exactly what they say they are – the minimum acceptable standards of performance for that activity. There is nothing complex about this but there is something slightly revolutionary about the idea.

Until recently, defining the expected performance was 'just not done'; people were assumed to know what was acceptable. But in today's highly competitive business environment it is no longer realistic to make assumptions about performance *of anything*. If companies are to deliver the goals they have set themselves, everyone must be aware of the expected performance at their *individual level*.

Relationship between MPS and compensation

The MPS for a job is the expected standard *for that person to keep their job*: performance-enhancing goals, set later, will govern whether they are eligible for promotion, a pay rise, a bonus, or some other reward. The MPS merely details the performance they must deliver to receive their contractual compensation package.

The operative word here is *contractual*. The individual contracts with the employer to deliver a specific performance against a specified list of responsibilities. The employer contracts with the individual that *if they deliver the*

MPS for the job, then they will be paid the contracted compensation.

Setting Minimum Performance Standards

To do this, you use a combination of common sense and asking those who already carry out similar work. With a great many activities that belong in job descriptions it is possible to set arbitrary and desirable MPS based on simple criteria. It is easy to set the MPS that monthly reports covering 'sales interviews' and 'sales made' must *be prepared and submitted within five working days of the end of the month*. Nor is it difficult to set an MPS for a clear-desk policy that *all documents should be locked away at the end of a day*. On the other hand, some MPS may require you to carry out a certain amount of research.

The best approach is to establish all the MPS you can without consultation and then ask your colleagues to review them. They may be able to offer more appropriate standards based on their experience and knowledge. You should also review the MPS with people who are already doing similar jobs as they can tell you what is practical and realistic.

5 Skills analysis – What skills are needed for the job

The next step is to determine all the skills that will be needed to carry out the job responsibilities to the required minimum performance standard.

These skills will fall into two categories: *hard* and *soft*. Hard skills such as mathematics, computing, using machinery, typing, etc., are about making or moving things and are generally the result of the person's education and the training courses they have attended. Soft skills such as interpersonal skills, communication (verbal and written), presentation skills, non-verbal communication (how to dress, move, body

17

language, etc.), leadership, management ability, and so on, are about understanding and working with people.

Once your list is complete, you will have two columns: hard, practical skills that are prerequisites and can be tested or observed or proven through qualifications; and soft skills, some of which are prerequisites and some of which will be 'nice to have'.

At this stage, you do not need to decide exactly how you will check whether the candidates have the soft skills but it is important to decide on what skills you want them to have. As with the MPS, have the list checked by your colleagues and anyone else who can make a useful input.

6 Reporting line – Who will be the manager?

In any business there is some sort of hierarchy just because there is always someone who is the boss and everyone has to account for their performance to someone. This hierarchy is generally called the reporting line.

In large organisations, the reporting line may have ten or more levels between the Chief Executive and the shop floor, while in small to medium-sized enterprises with around 20 to 500 people it is unlikely that there will be more than, say, three or four levels. In some small businesses there will be just two: the boss and everyone else. Figure 1.1 gives an example of a reporting line.

The number of levels is not important but what must be made totally clear is where the job fits within the system. The person who eventually fills the post must know exactly who is reporting to them, who their colleagues will be and who their boss is. They must also be made aware of who their boss reports to and so on up the line. In this way, the person will be able to fit in more quickly as their position

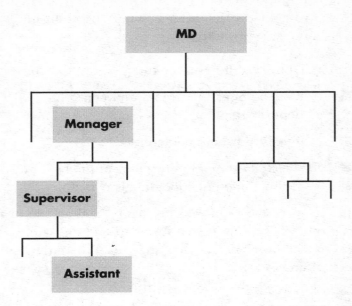

Fig.1.1 An example of an organisational diagram for the role of Assistant

in the corporate 'pecking order' is stated and any misconceptions as to rank or position can be dealt with.

In addition to knowing where the job fits into the greater scheme of things, the person applying for the position should also be given a brief corporate biography of their boss – and, if possible, of the boss's boss. This may sound radical but by establishing this brief biography a great deal of misunderstanding can be avoided. Here is an example from a software company:

> This position reports to VICKY EVANS who has been with the company for the last five years. She originally joined the design team and has subsequently been in all the major departments. She was the Head of Marketing before taking up her current position as Head of Design Technology. Vicky reports to DAVID WILLIS who is the Marketing Director, a job he has held for

the past three years, having joined the company from Abracadabra Software.

This biography establishes three things about the company:

- it encourages movement between departments
- it likes to promote internally
- it recruits straight into senior positions if no suitable internal candidate is available.

It also gives the candidate the names and a little of the background of their potential superiors and this will enable them to feel more at ease when they meet them during the selection process.

7 Compensation – How much does the job pay?

'The labourer is worthy of his hire' – but exactly what is a job really worth? Like everything else in business, the market has a major impact on what a particular job should pay: if you pay below market rates then you will not be able to attract the right candidates, if you pay above market rates then you risk attracting people who are only interested in what's in it for them.

Managerial positions

If you look around at the market, things are never simple. This morning's paper contained an advertisement that sought

Business Manager – Package to £70,000 + car

and down the page another was looking for

Senior Underwriter – c.$75,000 + Bonus, Tax free

a third wanted

Construction Manager – To £60,000 plus significant bonuses

and a fourth needed

Sales & Marketing Director – Competitive Salary + Car + Benefits

Finally, there was one that hedged its bets completely by stating

Managing Director – c.£80–100,000 + Profit share & Benefits

Not one of the advertisements stated what the basic salary was – and yet it is the basic salary that you are interested in. The overall package is important but to get the basic salary correct is an overwhelming priority. When it comes down to it, what the candidate really wants to know is how much they will be getting in pay each and every month.

Fortunately, there are ways of overcoming this lack of information. Various recruitment consultants publish statistics relating to managers' pay and similar information is often available through the various professional institutes, the large accountancy companies and the libraries of the larger university business schools.

Non-managerial positions

For non-managerial positions, the job advertisements in the local and national newspapers are an excellent source of pay scales – made more valuable by the fact that jobs are advertised under their functional job title so that you can get a direct comparison.

You will find that there is a range of basic salaries associated with a job. This range is dependent on where the job is located in the country, the size of the company, the business sector and the decision of management as to whether they wish to pay above the market average or below it.

Internal pay structures

Having acquired market data, you must then take into consideration the pay scales you already have within the company. If you are recruiting for a job that already exists, then a rate of pay for that job already exists and to move significantly from this risks unrest within your current staff. However, with a completely new role your benchmark is what others at the same level in the hierarchy are being paid.

Cash-flow cost

The cash-flow cost of paying a given salary must now be calculated. In most European countries, and many others around the world, a system of social security taxes exists whereby the employer has to pay a fixed percentage of the employee's salary as a tax. This cost is deductible in the company accounts but has a significant impact on the cash flow – it can add anything from 7% to 40% of gross basic salary, depending on the country where the job is located.

The rest of the package

Most companies recognise that they will have to invest more in their people than just the salary. Pensions, life assurance, private medical insurance, performance-related bonuses and holidays are all part of the modern compensation package.

Pensions

Just about everyone in work today belongs to a pension scheme. With the high degree of labour mobility, the attractiveness of company schemes is beginning to fade and many more people have their own private policy. Your company may or may not have established a company scheme and if it has, employees may or may not have to join the scheme. Either way, you should encourage your people to have some sort of retirement scheme in place.

The question is, who funds the pension? In most company schemes, the employer contributes a fixed percentage of the employee's basic salary – this contribution can be anything from 2% up to 20% depending on the scheme, the employer, and the employee's position in the hierarchy. The employee is often allowed (or even encouraged) to contribute as well.

Over the last few years, there has been a move away from company and 'final salary' schemes and employees are being encouraged to set up their own private schemes. In this case, the scheme has nothing to do with the company and the only contributor is the employee. Many companies now encourage their people to have private schemes as this relieves them of a financial burden (the contributions) and a long-term responsibility (the administration of the scheme, the investment of the money, and the payment of pensions). Companies who genuinely care about their employees recognise that this is disadvantageous to the employees and they compensate either by paying a higher salary or by arranging to make the contributions.

At its simplest level, provision of pension contributions is likely to add an additional 10% of basic salary to the cost of the remuneration package.

Life Assurance

Often referred to as 'death in service' benefits, life assurance has almost always been part of the pension scheme structure.

Designed to pay out a fixed multiple of the basic annual salary (say, 1.5–3 times), the scheme is there to provide a lump sum to the family or beneficiaries of the employee if the employee dies while involved in working for the company. A good scheme will provide cover during the time the person is employed – irrespective of whether they are at work, on holiday, travelling to and from work or at home. The candidate will certainly want to know whether you have such a scheme.

You will also need to consider a type of cover often referred to as 'key man insurance'. Such a policy is designed to pay out *to the company* if one of their employees dies. Normally restricted to senior managers and some other key personnel, this type of insurance will provide an immediate lump sum to the company to cover such things as the cost of recruitment of a replacement and temporary staff cover for the job.

Life assurance typically adds around 2% of basic salary to the overall costs plus more if 'key man insurance' is taken out.

Private Medical Insurance

Although the UK has a national health system that is free to all users, most other countries do not and there is a requirement to make regular monthly or quarterly payments to a private medical insurance scheme. There is even a tendency for more senior employees in the UK to expect private medical insurance. As medical insurance needs to be part of the overall remuneration package, and to cover all the immediate family, it adds to the overall cost of employment by, typically, a further 2%–4% of basic salary.

Performance-related bonuses

Some advocates of performance-related pay claim that it is possible to have all remuneration set this way but such thinking totally ignores some of the basics of motivation.

If a person feels that their security, and that of their family, is under threat – as might occur if they are being paid only on the basis of performance-related criteria – then their priority and commitment reverts from the company and their focus is on the family. On the other hand, if all their basic needs are taken care of through the basic salary then they will focus on the company's needs and be motivated to perform at a higher standard so that they can earn a bonus.

You must also remember that the company and the employee enter into a contract that says, in effect, that 'they agree to work to a certain standard and the company agrees to buy their labour from them at a certain rate'. This contractual base should not be tampered with. However, there is no reason why the base salary should not be set sufficiently low that it just covers the needs of the individual, the package including a performance-related bonus scheme that will allow them to achieve the level of income they feel they deserve, without limit.

Setting up a fair scheme that genuinely rewards performance is an extremely complex subject and you should seek advice from the consultants who specialise in compensation if you want to go down this route: if you get it wrong it can be a total and very expensive disaster.

Of course, performance-related pay should be self-funding. As with any payment made to an employee, there will be social security taxes to pay but at least you will not have to treat bonuses as a fixed overhead but as a variable expense of doing business.

Other add-on costs

Within any compensation package there are various additional benefits that you can make available should the circumstances demand – however, remember they will add to the cost of the job. These additional benefits include:

- company car – very popular in the UK but little used elsewhere

- school fees – unusual in a person's home country but often a key benefit if the person is working abroad

- relocation costs – relatively common if a person has to move house to take up a job

- mortgage guarantees – especially for senior staff.

Holidays

With some countries insisting on legislating on working conditions, it is not surprising that most companies are faced with providing each employee with a certain number of days' paid vacation as a statutory requirement. Whether legislation exists or not, a certain number of days' paid holiday is now the norm and this ranges from 10 working days in the USA to 30 working days in some continental European countries.

To this corporate holiday allowance you have to add the public holidays – these cover the major religious festivals plus the additional days written into law. The statutory public holidays range from 9 days per year in the UK to 15 days in such countries as Germany, Austria and Spain. For a full list of statutory holidays see the Appendix.

Of course, holiday entitlement does not add direct cost, but it does mean that the production or performance goals associated with each job will have to reflect that a person in, for example, Germany may work only 216 days even without sick leave or any one of the range of additional statutory days off (for house moving, bereavement, marriage, important family events, and so on) to which they may be entitled.

Total costs of the compensation package

Only a detailed and careful calculation will reveal the complete costs of a compensation package but, as a rough guide, the overhead cost of a job will be around 150% of basic salary per year plus the costs of additional benefits that the company choose to award either annually or as a one-off. Employing people is not cheap!

Back to the Job Description – the final bits

By now you have:

(i)   decided the functional job title and the corporate job title

(ii) determined the key and secondary responsibilities and their minimum performance standards

(iii) analysed and determined the hard and soft skills that you require a peson to have for this job

(iv) established the reporting line

(v)   decided on the basic salary and calculated the cost of the total compensation package, and

(vi) fixed the holiday entitlement and other terms and conditions.

Review the general job description

Now is the time to review the general job description that you wrote at the beginning of the process. At this stage there is likely to be a need to modify the description a little in light of the details but, in general, the description is likely to be accurate.

Write the job description

The final activity is to pull all the material together and to present it in one coherent, well-laid-out document that will be used by everyone involved in the selection process. This document will form the basis of the search for candidates, any advertisements will depend on the contents, it will assist the potential recruit in understanding what the job is about, and it will eventually form the basis of the contract between the company and the person you recruit.

Exactly what this document should look like is not important but it should be carefully reviewed by everyone involved to ensure there are no errors or omissions and that it contains all the seven items listed in the box on page 10. With this carefully prepared document to hand, you can now set about finding someone who will fulfil your requirements.

CHAPTER TWO

Finding the right person for the right job

With your carefully written job description to hand, you can start seeking the right person for the job. And the

RECRUITMENT CHECKLIST

1   Ensure the job description is complete

2   Identify sources of recruits

3   Decide on the approach to be used to attract applications

4   Review all curriculum vitae and letters received

5   Select an interview list

6   Carry out initial interviews

7   Select a shortlist (check skills)

8   Check all credentials and references

9   Carry out final interviews

10 Make the offer

11 The contract of employment

12 Inform others: unsuccessful candidates and company personnel

right person is the person with the skills and attributes that match those you have defined in the job description. You must keep this in mind at all times – selecting a person 'because they seem likely to fit in' or because 'they seem like a nice person' is important but, at this point, very much a secondary reason. The pressures on companies to succeed mean that they must focus their efforts on achieving their objectives and not on developing inappropriately recruited staff.

To ensure you select the right staff, you should establish a process for recruitment - using a checklist such as the one above – so that you are always reminded of what has to be done.

Use the job description

This is the document discussed in chapter one and which you have aleady prepared. Without this, the search will be almost impossible. At this stage, you should circulate the job description to all those who are to be involved in the recruitment process so that they can familiarise themselves with it. It is particularly important that the person to whom the job holder will report has a copy and has agreed it – after all, this is the person who must manage the new recruit and get them functioning productively as soon as possible.

Sources of recruits

There are a number of sources of potential recruits: your existing staff, people employed by other companies, the unemployed, and those about to leave full-time education and join the jobs market.

Existing staff

Many employers are reluctant to seek candidates from amongst their existing staff, arguing that this just doubles the workload associated with recruitment. While this appears true, it is also false thinking. An existing employee is unlikely to need as much training (if any) you already know a great deal about them, internal transfers encourage staff loyalty, and it might be easier to fill the place vacated by the transfer. These last two points are particularly important when you consider that the transfer may function as a promotion – which is motivational – and this means you will be looking for a person to fill a lower position, something that is often easier as there tends to be a greater pool of potential recruits.

It is often preferable to fill a position from within the company. Doing so signals to the existing staff that you are serious about development and that everyone has the opportunity to seek a promotion or a change. In today's company, with flatter organisational hierarchies, it is becoming increasingly difficult to provide promotion in the traditional sense of the word – there are not the jobs available at higher levels. On the other hand, a lateral move to a different position, possibly in a different section or department, provides a change and, for many people, this is as good as a promotion. This is particularly true of technical jobs – machinists, technicians, computer programmers – and of administrative jobs – secretarial, administration personnel, even managers.

Obviously, the change has to be attractive. This may mean that you have to provide a new compensation and employment package – perhaps an increase in pay or holiday entitlement in exchange for increased responsibilities – or maybe a change in corporate title will suffice. It is even possible that moving someone to a different location or office within the company is all that is needed for the job to become attractive.

People employed in other companies

Generally, the biggest source of potential candidates is the workforce of other companies.

As with all sources, there are advantages and disadvantages. On the positive side, you will be able to bring in new experience and skills, the person is probably already trained and it saves on the disruption that occurs with internal transfers. The introduction of 'new blood' can be very healthy, especially in management, and this can also be a way for the company to gain market knowledge. On the negative side, unlike the situation with internal candidates, you don't know the people, you are unlikely to know what work they have been doing and their performance in previous jobs is much harder to check. All this notwithstanding, recruiting from other companies is often the favoured approach and the best source of qualified candidates, especially for the more senior positions in the company.

The unemployed

There is a tendency to avoid recruiting from amongst the unemployed because they are often perceived as being somehow less suitable – 'After all, if they were any good, then they wouldn't be unemployed!' This is, of course, only partially true.

There are many people who are currently unemployed who are in the jobs market through no fault of their own. Company closures, bankruptcies, and downsizing have all put experienced and skilled candidates out of work. These people often approach new jobs with a very realistic attitude about their own skills and the value they can bring to a new employer. In addition, such candidates are likely to have prepared themselves well – CVs will be properly presented and fully up-to-date, they understand the selection process, they are readily available for interview and can start a new job without having to work out notice periods.

Of course, there are many people who are unemployed as a result of being fired from their jobs, as opposed to being made redundant, because of an infringement of their employment contract. You will need to check carefully the reasons why someone has left a job in these circumstances but this is something that should be a routine part of any job selection process.

Finally, there are the chronically, or long-term, unemployed – people who have been out of work for months, if not years. It is possible that the positions you have available may be just the thing to get these people back into useful employment. But this can present a major challenge – they are often so demoralised and negative that a very significant investment in their development would have to be made to obtain a satisfactory performance. Most companies cannot afford this level of investment in training. However, there are often grants and other forms of governmental assistance which may make taking on a long-term unemployed person possible – and attractive.

First-time job seekers

Finally, there are those coming into the market for the first time – students and school leavers who have finished their education and are seeking their first job.

There is a paradox here – people with no work experience bring little added value to a company but they cannot gain the necessary experience until they have a job. In the circumstances, do you recognise their university and college qualifications and give them a responsible job, or do you recognise their lack of experience and only recruit them to lower-level positions? This is not an easy decision to make – there are many examples in which companies have recruited graduates (especially those with MBAs) and put them in management positions only to have them fail to deliver the expected performance due to lack of experience and inadequate skills in managing people. Another disadvantage is that first-time candidates are unlikely to stay very long – they will gain experience and move to another company for a higher paying job and you end up having invested in the training of other people's staff.

Unless your company has the ability and capacity to undertake long-term development, it is unwise to allow good academic qualifications to outweigh the need for experience and interpersonal skills.

Attracting applications

Having decided where you are going to look for recruits, you now have to determine how you are going to attract the right people. And when you have the right people, you will need to be able to compare them with each other in a fair manner. This requires a standardised format for the information.

Most companies request a curriculum vitae. Unfortunately, these documents are likely to come in a huge variety of formats and with inconsistent content that makes comparisons difficult. It makes sense, therefore, to have an application form that is either completed by the candidate or entered directly into a database so that the presentation of the information is consistent.

Job application forms

Only you can decide what information you need; however, the application form in Figures 2.1 and 2.2 contains the basics. Make sure you have provided adequate space for each answer – especially for the sections on work history and educational qualifications.

Some people may resist supplying information in all sections, arguing that an employer has no right to ask for details concerning the private life of the applicant. Their argument is based on the fact that the law states that discrimination on the basis of gender or ethnic background is illegal and that questions on marital status and number of dependants are discriminatory. While discrimination is wrong, employers do need to know the gender and marital status (and, possibly, the number of dependants as this has an impact on such things as life assurance (death-in-service benefits), mobility, and other employment conditions.

Contacting internal candidates

There are two types of internal recruit: those who are put forward by management and those who respond to an internal advertisement.

The first step is to circulate the job description to all managers and to request they submit all potential candidates. This will bring you a selection of people: some will be suitable, some will be there because the manager wants to get rid of them for under-performance and some will be there because the manager cannot work with them. This mixed bag will then have to be sorted out.

Irrespective of the reason that the managers have put them forward, the candidates must all be treated in the same way. CVs must be read, the candidates' latest annual appraisals need to be reviewed, and the managers need to be interviewed to find out why they have put a person forward.

Internal advertising

You should also advertise the job internally. This will expose all the staff to the details of the job so that everyone has the opportunity of applying. In this way those people who are suitable but have not been put forward by their managers for whatever reason will have a chance to be considered.

The internal job advertisement must be prepared with the same care as you would use for an external advertisement. It is not sufficient to announce

Secretary required for logistics department

or

Sales Manager, northern region, needed

Acme Widget Engineering
Employment Application Form

All candidates are requested to complete this application form in BLOCK CAPITALS. The form is designed to act as a summary and to allow us to collect all the information we require in a common format for easy reference.

Personal Details:

Family name: _____ Title: (Mr, Mrs, Miss, Ms, Dr) _____

First names in full: _____

Current address: _____

_____

_____

Private telephone: _____ Fax: _____

Date of Birth: _____ Nationality: _____

Gender: MALE/FEMALE   Status: SINGLE/MARRIED/DIVORCED

Dependants: YES/NO _____

Mobility: (Willingness to move and work where required): YES/NO

Education and Qualifications:

University/College: _____

From   To

Degree/Diploma and Subject: _____

_____

Secondary School: _____

From   To

Examinations and Subjects: _____

_____

_____

Professional Memberships: _____

_____

Fig. 2.1 The front of a typical application form

Acme Widget Engineering
Employment Application Form

Complete in chronological order with your most recent position first.
Please give the dates of employment, your function and a brief description of the work done.

Employment History:

Current Employer: _____

                   From: _____

Current Position/Function: _____

Brief Description of the Work: _____

_____

_____

_____

Employer: _____

           From: _____   To: _____

Position/Function: _____

Brief Description of the Work: _____

_____

_____

Employer: _____ From: _____ To: _____

Position/Function: _____

Brief Description of the Work: _____

_____

_____

_____

Please continue on a further sheet if required.

Fig. 2.2 The reverse of a typical application form

and assume that everyone will know what is required. You need to approach this by telling people what is really wanted. For example:

> Due to the departure of Jenny Smith at the end of next month, we need a secretary to take over her responsibilities in the Logistics Department. Reporting directly to Mr Jones, Head of Logistics, the secretary will be responsible for maintaining all the records, preparing movement orders, and handling all enquiries concerning documentation. We want to select someone for this role as soon as possible so that they can receive the appropriate training before Jenny leaves. The pay and conditions for the job are that of Senior Secretary.

This advertisement tells everyone who is being replaced, it identifies the boss, outlines the key responsibilities and states the pay and conditions.

Here is one for a new role:

> Due to the successful expansion of the sales team, we are now looking to appoint a Sales Manager for the northern region. This person will report to Barry Davis, the Sales Director, and will have a team of five people reporting to him or her. This is a new position and the key responsibilities are to further enhance the performance of the sales team and to increase the sales from the region. The pay and conditions for the job are that of Section Manager.

Again, the advertisement outlines the key responsibilities, the reporting line, the pay and conditions and why this position is being advertised. In each case, of course, you would add how, and to whom, interested candidates should apply.

The actual method of advertising internally will be determined by the company's existing method of communicating with the staff – noticeboards, internal newsletters, e-mail and circulation of memos are all possibilities and experience shows that all bring forward candidates, with noticeboards being the least effective and direct contact being the most effective.

In general, internally advertised positions attract a good response that tends to come in without the necessary documentation – people talk to the contact person and say they are interested. This requires you to review their 'personnel' file (the CV, appraisals, and so on) without which you cannot make an appropriate decision. This is where application forms are useful.

Attracting external candidates

Lower to junior management positions

For jobs ranging from the lower end of the skills range up to and including junior management levels, the usual approach is to place a display advertisement in the Situations Vacant section of the local newspapers and trade journals. The size of the advertisement can be critical – a large display gives the impression that this is a serious and important job whereas a small non-display says that this is a lowly position. The format and layout of the advertisement can be copied from those already appearing but the content needs to be carefully thought out.

The most effective advertisements are those that state clearly the name of your company, the functional title of the job being advertised, the pay range and a brief description based on that in the job description itself. You should then include specific instructions about how to apply – for example, they should send an application letter plus a CV or they should work or call you for an application form. You should also require them to quote a reference number if you are advertising more than one job at that time.

Acme Widget Engineering Sales Manager, Northern England

Anytown, Workshire   £21,000 p.a. + car

Due to the successful expansion of the sales team, we are now looking to appoint a Sales Manager for the north of England. The successful candidate will report to the Sales Director and will have a team of five people reporting to him or her. This is a new position and the key responsibilities are to further enhance the performance of the sales team and to increase the sales from the region.

To apply please send a full CV and letter of application to John Smith, Personnel Director, Acme Widget Engineering Ltd, Engineers Drive, Anytown, Workshire.

Fig. 2.3 An advertisement for press publication. Note that the style and content matches the internal advertisement for the same job given on p. 38.

For maximum impact you should place the same advertisement in all the local papers covering your area, including the 'freebies'. In addition, you should copy the advertisement onto cards and have them displayed at the local Job Centres. In this way you will cover all the potential candidates whether they are currently employed or unemployed. If you wish to attract school leavers, then placing the advertisement with the school's careers office can also be effective, especially if your search is taking place towards the end of the school year.

Finally, word of mouth is effective. Give all your staff a copy of the advertisement and ask them to spread the word. This is powerful – if your current staff is happy and committed to the company then they will only suggest the job to people who they think will fit in with the company and thus a certain amount of preselection is being done. Obviously, if you have discontented staff this is not an approach to be recommended.

More senior positions

For more senior positions, especially those in management, you really have a choice of three methods: press advertising, word of mouth and using an executive search consultant (head hunter).

Advertising and word of mouth

The construction of the press advertisement is the same as for any other job you might advertise, but you would place it in national newspapers and trade journals rather than local ones. Unfortunately, although press advertising is very popular, it is not as successful at senior level as you might imagine. There is evidence that the press can attract quality candidates but it is noteworthy that around 70% of all senior positions are filled by candidates who have *not* responded to such advertisements.

This seems paradoxical – why advertise a job that is likely to be filled by someone who does not respond? The resolution of the paradox is that, by advertising, you broadcast that the company is looking for a candidate and you might just attract someone of the right calibre; in addition, when it becomes known you are looking this will trigger applications through networking and word of mouth.

Word of mouth is as powerful, if not more so, when recruiting for senior management roles than it is at the other end of the workforce. Your management colleagues will know managers and they will certainly pass the word to those who they think might fit in. And they are not going to tell anyone who they feel is not the sort of person that they want to work with. Again, a process of selection is taking place. Besides using your colleagues to spread the word, you can also let people know by mentioning the vacancy when talking to other business people whenever you meet them in a professional or social environment.

Head hunters

More correctly know as executive search consultants, head hunters are professional organisations specialising in locating and pre-screening candidates for senior management or technical positions. They are expensive in that a successful search will result in you having to pay a fee of around one to one-and-a-half times the annual salary of the position being filled. On the other hand, if they are not successful the only fee you should have to pay is for any advertising they have done. This performance-related approach means that they really will work for you.

Given that you are going to have to pay, why use a search consultant? The usual reasons are (i) you haven't the time, (ii) you haven't the expertise, (iii) the position is too critical for any personal preferences to be allowed, and (iv) you do not want the 'market' to know that you are looking for a senior manager.

A search consultant will require a copy of the job description plus information about the activities of the company. They may also need to know why you are looking to fill the position – for example, if the company is in difficulty and you really need a 'turn round' expert, they will need to know this. The consultant will then undertake an extensive interview with you so that they can identify all the constraints, requirements, preferences and conditions associated with the job. They will then need to decide whether they can undertake the search.

With the search assignment agreed, the consultant will normally take two actions: the first is that they will place a display advertisement in the appropriate newspaper (where they are unlikely to mention the name of the company), and the second is to review their very extensive databases for potential candidates who might meet the search criteria. The advertisement will attract possible applicants who may be looking for a career move, while the database is likely to identify people who may not currently be looking for a change. Obviously, this latter group has to be approached very carefully indeed as the intention is to 'poach' the person and get them to join your company.

Having identified a number of potential candidates, the consultant will then underake a selection process to put together a shortlist of genuinely suitable candidates. In this way, you will be presented only with those who would be able to do the job. The CVs of the shortlist plus the consultant's own report on each candidate will then be forwarded to you for consideration. The consultant will then assist you by setting up the initial interviews and may even attend the meetings. Once a candidate has been identified for the position, the consultant will handle the offer and may even assist with the contract. Only when the candidate has actually taken up the position and has completed a probationary period (six to twelve months) does the full fee become due.

CVs and letters of application

One of the most time-consuming activities connected with recruitment is reading the application letters and CVs. There are plenty of horror stories around of how personnel managers and recruitment consultants never read beyond the first paragraph of the letter or never read beyond the name and address on the CV, but this is not a route you can take. Reading the documents sent is the only way you will identify potential candidates.

As this is going to take some time, you should send a brief letter to each applicant thanking them for their interest and advising them that they will hear from you again within three to six weeks – or longer in the case of management appointments. This letter is a courtesy that serves two purposes: firstly it will stop the applicant bothering you, and secondly it keeps them interested in the company.

Ease of understanding

There are numerous books available on how to write an application letter and how to prepare the perfect CV. However, unfortunately for their authors, and for you, most job applicants have not bought the books. As a result the letters and CVs can make almost impenetrable reading. Make an initial selection based on letters and CVs that look visually appealing, are well laid out, and are legible – care in preparation of letters and CVs is likely to demonstrate similar attention to detail in the person's work. All the others should be put aside at this stage – you may need to come back to them later. Some people may say it is unfair to select in this way – it may be, but anyone who chooses not to take the time and make the effort to present themselves in an attractive and easy-to-understand manner is also likely to show a similar lack of care in their work.

Completeness of information

This first group of applications should be reviewed for completeness of information. Almost all will lack some small details but you should be looking for completeness of personal details and work history. Educational qualifications should also be in the application but if a person left school without qualifications and never attended a college then this should be noted but not necessarily held against them unless it disqualifies them on the basis of the job specification.

Any applications with serious omission should now be put to one side for the time being and you should concentrate your attention on the remaining documents.

Are they suitable? The interview list

Now read through all the documents and see what the applicant is offering. A checklist is useful so that you can match the candidate's skills and experience with the job description. To avoid duplication of effort you should focus on the specifications and the easiest method is to draw up a form that lists the prerequisite skills and experience down the left and has space on the right for you to note against it what the applicant is offering.

Some personnel and recruitment specialists recommend that each application be given a reference number and that only that number should appear on the checklist. This is so that, when you compare applicants, you do so without being influenced by any other information – this is the same principle as the 'blind tasting' of wines in which labels, place of origin, grape varieties and so on do not influence the tasting process. This approach has considerable value if you have a lot of applicants.

At this stage, you should check to see if you have sufficient applications that match your requirements to produce an interview list of, say, six to ten people. If not, then you will need to go back to the applications that had missing information and, possibly, to those put aside because they were not easy to read. If you do have enough suitable applications, you can move to the next stage: interviewing the candidates.

CHAPTER THREE

Recruiting the right person for the right job

Once you have six to ten suitable applicants, all of whom more or less meet your written specifications, you are ready to start the interview procedure.

The initial interview

You should use the telephone to set up the initial interviews – this is for two practical reasons: (i) since unsuccessful applicants need to be contacted within a certain timeframe, you need to get through the initial interview stage as fast as possible, and (ii) it allows you to make an assessment of what each applicant sounds like on the telephone – remember, they will be unprepared for the call and, as a result, you will hear the 'real' person.

You should plan on each interview taking 45 minutes to one hour and they should be spaced at least 45 minutes apart. There are practical reasons for this: 45–60 minutes is long enough to make an initial assessment and to obtain the 'missing' information; and you will need at least 30 minutes to write up your interview notes and 15 minutes to review the CV and letter of the next applicant. In addition, it is a courtesy that is all too often ignored that job applicants should not have to meet each other when competing for a position.

Practical arrangements

Everyone has their own style for dealing with meetings – some like to have a secretary bring the candidate to the interview room, others like to go and fetch them; some like to use their office for the meeting, others prefer to use a conference room. There is no hard-and-fast rule as to what works best but there are some interesting psychological factors that come into play.

Asking a secretary to collect the applicant, while giving you extra time and establishing you as someone with a secretary, actually induces extra stress in the applicant who is probably feeling nervous as it is. If you collect the applicant it helps them relax, it makes the whole process less pressurised and more informal, and allows you to observe the person outside of the interview situation. A relaxed applicant is more likely to respond openly, which will make things move along more smoothly.

On the other hand, the 'secretary' can provide additional feedback on how the applicant reacts to a 'junior' member of staff – were they nervous, were they polite, did they ask pertinent questions about the company? This can be useful even though it may deliver the applicant in a more stressed frame of mind – especially if they are unused to dealing with secretaries.

Using an office or a meeting room also produces some interesting effects. Your office may or may not impress the applicant – remember, you and the company are being assessed at the same time as you are assessing the applicant. Your office may be very grand and extremely tidy, or small and untidy – both say a great deal about you and the company. To avoid this problem, you could, and perhaps should, use the more neutral surroundings of a meeting room.

Where you and the applicant sit is also critical. Facing the person across the desk is stress-inducing and confrontational and is likely to leave the applicant uncomfortable and on edge. Again, you need the person to relax and be open and it is wise, therefore, to position the two of you so that the desk or table is not between you. Sitting across the corner of the table is generally best as this minimises the barrier while still leaving you with a table for your papers.

There are many people who prefer to interview seated in chairs around a coffee table. While this is the ultimate in informal arrangements, it does have certain disadvantages: (i) both of you are trapped into a semi-reclining position, and (ii) if the applicant is of the opposite gender from you they may well feel additionally discomforted by the intimacy such an arrangement may suggest.

In general, therefore, you should collect the candidate yourself, use a meeting room with a table and sit across the corner – this approach is the most suitable for the circumstance.

Interview content and procedure

The purpose of the initial interview is not to select the person for the job, but to select a shortlist of candidates who can then be interviewed in depth. You are looking for options from which to make a final choice.

Having carefully reviewed the letter of application and the CV or application form before the meeting, you will have noted the 'missing' information and the areas that need clarification and you will have prepared a list of questions you want answering. The first step is to collect all the information you need and for this it is best to use direct, 'closed' questions that require a specific answer. This process will help the applicant to settle and relax.

The initial interview is also the time to allow the applicant to sell themselves to you and this must be encouraged. They will need to know about the company (unless they are existing staff), the details of the job, and anything else they feel uncertain about. This enables them to assess whether they would want to work for you (which is as critical as you wanting to employ them) and, at the same time, they will be able to tell you how, in their opinion, they match your requirements.

INITIAL INTERVIEW CHECKLIST

1   Arrange the interviews

2   Arrange suitable facilities

3   Prepare thoroughly by reviewing letter, CV and application form

4   Have a checklist of missing information and questions

5   Collect the applicant when they arrive

6   Help them relax by collecting the missing information

7   Tell them about the company and the job and answer their questions

8   Ask the key questions

9   Arrange for copies of qualifications and details of referees

10 Tell the applicant what will happen next

11 Escort the applicant out

12 Write up the interview report

Then you can start to explore the other areas of importance. Here, the key questions are: (a) why are they looking for a career move? (This should also cover why they are looking to leave their current employer.) And (b) what added value do they feel they can bring to your company? If asking these open-ended questions outright seems a little blunt, then preface them by asking the applicant to give you a brief overview of their work history and what they feel they have achieved as a result.

Throughout the interview, you should adopt an open, friendly position – relaxed but not laid-back – a position that encourages the candidate to talk naturally and openly about themself. When they ask questions you should answer them as fully as possible without revealing commercially senstive information. The interview should be quietly professional, with a firm focus on finding out what you need to know in the shortest possible time without giving the appearance of being in a hurry. The interview may be routine to you, but to the candidate it is a big step in their career and you should make it as easy as possible for them. Although the old-fashioned 'tough' interviews are singularly out of place in a modern commercial environment that is seeking motivated and top-quality employees, that does not mean you should allow the meeting to be an overly friendly social chat. Keep focused and keep the meeting moving along.

Once you and the candidate have exchanged all the necessary information, you can now turn to the administrative aspect of what happens next. You should ask the applicant to provide you with copies of all their academic and vocational qualifications so that you can check them. You should also ask for the name and address of a professional referee – this could be the person they currently work for or someone else in the company – and at least one personal referee who has known them for some years. You should tell the candidate that the references will be checked if the applicant is selected for the final shortlist, but reassure them that if this is likely to present problems with their current employer then you will hold off on this until the very last moment. But do remember, the time to check the references is *before* you enter into a contract of employment: you will be offering the position subject to satisfactory references.

The final step is to tell the applicant how many people have been selected for initial interview and when they will hear from you as to the result of this interview.

Having escorted the applicant out, you must then write up an interview report while things are still fresh in your mind. This is not the time to make judgements, but it is the time to record your impressions of the applicant as a person and how they presented themself. Judgements as to suitability will come once you have finished all the interviews and can analyse the results.

Selecting the shortlist

Having completed all the initial interviews, you are now in the position to review all the applicants to see which ones match the criteria you have established. This is a purely analytical task to start with.

Using the checklist prepared when you drew up the initial interview list, work your way through the job description again to double-check that you have listed all the prerequisite skills and attributes and then check what is being offered by the applicant. This is a more detailed analysis than first carried out and you will need to use the interview report to assist in obtaining all the details. Some recruitment specialists allocate a numerical value to the skills and attributes with the prerequisites attracting values that are commensurate with their importance. This allows you to grade the applicant's skill and allocate a value. For example, if you consider that having more than five years of experience as a lathe operator is worth five points, and the applicant has four years of experience, then you would allocate four points. This sort of grading analysis can be very useful, especially when dealing with very similarly qualified applicants.

There is no fixed rule how many candidates you should call for a second interview and the decision must be based on the analysis of each applicant's skills and attributes in comparison with the job description. It is likely that the initial interview and analysis will have reduced the numbers, but do not be restrictive: it is possible that all the applicants should reappear on the shortlist of candidates.

Check credentials

Now is the time to start the process of checking the qualifications, references and other statements made by the applicant in their CV. You may well feel that this is unnecessary but it is only by checking that you will be able to see if the applicant has been telling the truth. There are many reports of people who have lost good jobs because someone has checked and found that they had been rather economical with the truth at interview.

Qualifications and previous jobs

Academic and vocational qualifications can be checked by examining the certificates issued and, if there is any remaining doubt, you can call the examining body and give them the applicant's details, the name and year of the qualification and ask them to provide verification. Experience shows this step is not often necessary as the certificates generally show clearly what qualifications have been obtained. However, care must be taken when the certificate is for a higher qualification (such as a degree) and is issued by a little known or unknown university – an area of fraud in recent years.

Most of the other statements made in the CV are also easily verifiable – often just by making a phone call to the relevant company to confirm that the person did work there and did hold the position claimed. If the company is very small or unknown to you then a check with a reference agency such as Dun & Bradstreet or by a search at Companies House will tell you a great deal about the company, including whether it still exists and, if not, who its successors are. This will again allow you to contact someone for verification of the applicant's details.

References

Finally, you should contact the referees. The personal reference generally presents no problem – people usually call on friends or public figures such as a minister, a police officer, a member of the judiciary or a business person to act as a personal reference. The professional reference, on the other hand, can be fraught with problems: some employers will only provide a neutral reference confirming that a person has worked or does work for the company and the position they held or hold. Other companies will provide more detail but are unlikely to reveal how the person has performed – and few will ever reveal if the person was dismissed for criminal activities. This pushes the onus back on you to check by other means – perhaps by using a specialist investigation agency.

The final problem is generally that the applicant has not told their employer that they are seeking a career move and a request for a reference is thus likely to cause problems for the applicant, especially if they are unsuccessful in obtaining the new position. While you must tread carefully here, it is necessary that you have the reference *before* a job offer can be made and that means *before* a final interview. Because of the problems, many companies shy away from finding a solution, especially when the most obvious thing is to carry out a discreet investigation. The applicant can often assist by giving you permission for the investigation – especially since having to carry one out is as much to protect their current job as to protect you.

Although understandable, it is not desirable to leave this situation unresolved, especially when the position is in senior management. Fortunately, there are specialists in this field and it is worth employing one to conduct the necessary research. Of course, if you are using a head hunter, they will have already addressed the problem. If the position you wish to fill is very senior indeed, then you may also wish to carry out a more thorough investigation involving credit checking, police record, and so on. Again, use a professional for this and always tell the applicant what is being investigated and allow them to see the report produced – or, at least, the summary.

Reconfirm the short list

Having done all the analysis of skills and experience, and having checked all the details and references, you will now have your final shortlist. The applicants will have been checked out: they are all qualified and they are all suitable in terms of the job description criteria. Now you must see if they really will fit.

The only tasks that remain are: (i) to confirm they have the skills you want (and that they claim to have), and (ii) to find out which of the candidates your colleagues believe will contribute most to the company. Both these activities are part of the final interview.

Set up the final interviews

At this point, a little formality should be introduced to indicate the seriousness of this next step. Candidates for the final interview should be informed by letter, giving a date that allows them enough time to prepare and to request the necessary time off from their current employment. The letter should also state what is to happen, what the candidate should bring, and how long the process is likely to take. See Figure 3.1.

As you will be involving your colleagues in the final

selection process, it is likely that the interviews will take around half a day and any test or demonstration of skills will add further time. It might be fair, therefore, to request that the candidates make themselves available for a whole day. Although this may seem excessive, it is worthwhile as it ensures you have adequate time for the selection process. In addition, most candidates will have requested a full day off work and you should make good use of their commitment to the process. With a shortlist of four or five, this means you and your colleagues are going to be involved for substantial parts of four or five days.

It is also worthwhile requesting that the candidates supply a passport-sized photograph for the file to act as an *aide mémoire*. This is especially valuable if there are a lot of candidates on the shortlist.

Dear ... (*applicant's name*)
Private and Confidential
I am very pleased to inform you that you have been selected to attend a final interview for the position of ... (*functional title*) ...

The interview will take place at our offices, where we met before, and will take place on ... (*date*) ... at 0900 hrs. The interview process will last all day and we will, of course, provide you with lunch.

During the day you will be interviewed by ... (*names of two colleagues*) ... and ... (*the person who will be the new boss*) ... who is the person this position reports to. We will also expect you to undertake a number of tests so that you can demonstrate the skills that are of most importance in this position.

Please bring with you any documentary evidence or examples of your work ... (*use wording that is appropriate*) ... along with one passport-sized photograph of yourself for our records.

Please confirm by telephone that this appointment is convenient, I look forward to seeing you then.

Fig. 3.1 An invitation to a final interview

If, in attending this interview, the candidate will incur significant costs of travel or overnight accommodation, you would include a sentence to the effect that reasonable travel expenses would be reimbursed.

The final interview

The success of the final interview process is dependent on thorough preparation. Rooms for the interviews need to be checked and arranged, the day's schedule needs to be drawn up and circulated to all those involved, the candidate's file needs to be circulated in advance, interview report forms need to be designed and produced and arrangements need to be made for providing lunch for the candidate and paying any expenses they may have incurred.

These practical arrangements are self-evident but what is often forgotten is that you must also thoroughly brief each person involved in the interviews and you must set up the necessary skill tests.

Briefing the interviewers

Very few people are involved in recruitment interviewing as part of their normal work and, if they are, it will be infrequent. As a result, it is necessary to provide some guidelines on conducting the interview, especially on what each interviewer should be looking for.

A good guide is to use a senior manager from a different functional department as one of the interviewers. If you have a mentoring programme in operation (see Part Three), this person will probably take on the role of mentor or 'godfather/godmother' once the candidate is employed. (The function of these roles is explained in detail later in this book.) This person should be briefed to explore in some detail why the candidate is leaving their present job, why they think they want to work for your company, and what they feel they will bring in terms of added value. This is, essentially, a re-run of your questions from the initial interview.

The second interviewer should be, if possible, the senior functional manager for the department in which the position is located. This time, the focus of the interview should be on exploring in greater detail the work background and experience, to determine the overall potential of the candidate to develop and contribute to the company.

The final interview should be with the line manager, the person to whom the candidate will report if they are successful in getting the job. Here, a slightly different approach should be used – the interviewer should explain in detail how the team is constructed, what the work entails, the pressures and constraints encountered and what the candidate will be expected to do. The line manager should answer the candidate's questions openly and probe to see whether they think the candidate will fit in with the team *as a person*. This interview may also involve taking the candidate to meet the team, to see the work environment, and to tour the business premises.

Each interviewer must also be briefed on the interview reports that will be necessary and on the timing and format of the final selection meeting.

Skills tests

You cannot afford to make assumptions about a person's skills based on what you have been told or have found out – you must arrange for the candidate to demonstrate those skills.

This is relatively easy to do with practical skills such as operating machinery, typing, computer operations, technician work, driving, stores operations, but is somewhat more complicated with the soft skills associated with managing people.

In testing practical skills, it is wise to ask the candidate to undertake a practical demonstration under the watchful eyes of the head of the section in which the job will be and of someone doing the job already. For example, if the job is for a fork-lift truck driver in the stores then the head store man and the chief fork-lift truck driver should supervise. If the job is as a computer operator, then the IT manager and the senior operator should supervise. Besides the practical tests you may also wish to conduct oral and written tests to check on associated knowledge. A good example of this is the Health and Safety rules that apply in various parts of a business. It is entirely possible that you will need to set up a series of such tests so that a thorough assessment of the candidates' abilities and knowledge can be carried out – this is not only to help select the right person but also to act as a benchmark evaluation for the training programme.

Testing interpersonal and management skills

Testing the 'soft' skills associated with managing people is rather more difficult. Obviously, you can ask the candidate how they would handle a given situation but this does not allow you to see the skills in action. To overcome this problem, many companies are now turning to the use of assessment exercises administered by professional trainers. These exercises are mini case-studies in which each candidate is faced with a particular problem and asked to deal with it. The problems can range from being suddenly faced by an irate person who assumes that the candidate works for the company, to answering the telephone and having to deal with a staff member, to watching and analysing video recordings of situations. The candidate should also be questioned in detail about the behaviour that they might choose in a particular situation.

Finally, there is a growing use of psychometric profiles and attitude testing, all of which reveal the strengths and weaknesses of the candidate. Obviously, such testing must only be carried out by someone trained in the administration and interpretation of such tests – this normally means bringing in a consultant, but it is an investment worth making.

In particularly sensitive management positions – especially when the candidate will be at a very senior level, possibly even on the board – this testing of interpersonal and people-management skills may take a lot longer than a day. It is entirely possible that you would invite the candidate to the business premises for two or three days and invite them to sit in on various meetings, to talk to a range of senior managers, and to socialise with those who might be their future colleagues. Given the importance of competence and the ability to fit in with the team, this time is a good investment. Working with a person for two or three days of carefully structured situations and receiving feedback from all those involved will soon tell you whether the person will fit. It will also reveal the person's interpersonal skills in a way that is almost impossible in an interview situation.

Again, this testing process will also reveal the areas of weakness and will act as a benchmark evaluation for future training.

Making the final decision

As each candidate reaches the end of the interview and assessment process they should be told how many people are being interviewed and when they will be told the result. You should take care that you leave yourself enough time to make the decision, offer the job and have it accepted. If it is not accepted by your first choice, then it will have to be offered to the second choice – all of which takes time. A good guide is to say that they will be notified of the result within three weeks of the final candidate being interviewed.

To meet even this apparently relaxed time constraint

means that you and all those involved in the evaluation process will have to meet and make a decision very rapidly. Feedback from the people evaluating the skills and knowledge will have to be obtained so that you can confirm the skills you require are really there – and if they are not, or are weak, then you will have to decide whether an investment in training is worthwhile. You will need to collect in the interview reports and to analyse them. In all cases, the reports should contain an evaluation sheet with the specific skills, attitudes and competencies on it that the interviewer or evaluator was asked to check. The evaluation might be in the form 'the candidate has/has not got the skill' or you may choose to have a numerical value allocated. For example:

> Ability to collect pallets and to stack them neatly using the fork-lift truck:
> Very good (5) Good (4) Acceptable (3) Poor (2) Low (1) Non-existent (0)

The numerical approach is much more useful as it also contributes towards the benchmarks for training and it allows you to choose between candidates who appear, superficially, to offer the same.

With all the information in, it is possible that you have one outstanding candidate and the final decision is self-evident. This is not often the case in reality. Everyone has strengths and weaknesses and it is more likely that you will have two or three candidates, all of whom have scored highly but all of whom have some area of weakness. This is where you call a selection meeting.

The selection meeting

Before the meeting, circulate the files of the candidates who are 'in the frame' and have the potential to be offered the job. Each file should have a summary sheet that clearly shows how the candidate has been rated against all the criteria in the job description and should include the evaluations of all the interviewers.

All the interviewers must attend the meeting if a decision is not self-evident as a team decision has to be made. This is not the time to accept written recommendations as you will need to question each interviewer carefully so that a consensus can be reached. If you are looking at more than one candidate at this stage, then they should be ranked in order of preference.

Generally, the selection meeting can reach a decision on a candidate, who can then be offered the job. But occasionally the correct decision is to reject all the candidates and to start again. This is a tough decision as a lot of time and effort has gone into the process, but it is one that must be made if none of the candidates meets your requirements. In which case, you must review the job description and start all over again with a new advertisement that 'qualifies' the candidates more strictly.

Making the offer

With the decision made, you can now make a formal offer of the job. The successful candidate should be sent an offer letter to which you have attached a copy of the job description and a legally drawn up contract of employment. (See Figure 3.2.) These three documents must contain all the information concerning the job, the compensation package and the terms and conditions of employment including all the benefits (life assurance, pension, holidays, etc.) and any probationary period and training requirements. You should also include a formal statement of when you expect the candidate to have accepted the job and when they should start work. With all this to hand, the candidate can make their own evaluation about the job and can reach a decision.

It is very possible that the candidate will need clarification of some of the terms in the contract of employment and you must be willing to provide this. Some things may be negotiable and these should be clearly marked. In both cases, you may need a further meeting to agree the details.

Once this process is complete, you must receive a written confirmation that the candidate has accepted the job and, of course, a signed contract of employment. The process is now complete and a legal contract has been entered into which shows that the candidate is undertaking to do the job concerned to a specified standard and you are undertaking to compensate them for doing so.

The candidate should tell you in their acceptance letter (a) that they have notified their employer that they are leaving and (b) what period of notice they have to work out. Most employers expect either a week or a month depending on whether the person is paid weekly or monthly. Some more senior positions may require up to three months. This notice period is there to allow the employer to recruit a replacement and thus not be too inconvenienced. This notice period is often used by the candidate to take any unused holiday entitlement and there are many employers who encourage this on the basis that once a person has decided to leave they will no longer be fully committed to the current job. Depending on the type of work being done, the notice period may be foregone and the person immediately paid off for holiday and other compensation entitlements. This is common where the existing job allows the person access to commercially sensitive information.

Once you know the leaving conditions being applied, you should write a second letter confirming the date on which you expect the new employee to start work. You would also state the time they are to come to their new work location and to whom they have to report. Since holiday entitlement is generally governed by the length of time a person has worked for the company, if the new member of staff is recruited externally and your contract

Dear ... (*applicant*)

Private and Confidential

I am very pleased to be able to say that you have been successful in final interview for the position of ... (*functional title*) ... and I now formally offer this position to you.

I enclose two copies of our Employment Contract which includes the Job Description and the Terms & Conditions of Employment. Please read these carefully and, if you have no further questions, please sign *both* copies and return them to me within 10 working days. I will arrange for them to be counter-signed on behalf of the company and one copy will be returned to you. If you do have any questions about the contract, or anything else, please call me on ... (*phone number*) ... and I will be happy to answer them.

We are looking forward to you joining the company and I expect you to start work on ... (*specific date*) ... at ... (*time*) ... On that day, please bring with you any documents relating to social security and income tax (such as P45) that your current employer will provide.

When you arrive at the company on ... (*specific date*) ... please ask the receptionist to contact me so that I can introduce you to your new colleagues.

Yours sincerely,

John Smith
Personnel Director

Enc. 2x Employment Contract

Fig. 3.2 An example of an offer letter

allows for no holiday entitlement until completion of the probationary period, you should encourage them to take a short holiday before reporting to the new job. This also means they will be refreshed when they start.

Informing others: unsuccessful candidates and company personnel

Unsuccessful candidates

As soon as the job has been accepted and the contracts signed, you must write to each of the unsuccessful short-listed candidates informing them that they have not been successful. If they were good quality people, you should also tell them that you will keep their files and will contact them again if anything else suitable comes up. In this way you will be taking the first step towards building your own database of potential recruits.

With all the shortlist informed, now is the time to write to all the other applicants and tell them the bad news. And it is vital that this is done before the new person appears on their first day. If internal applicants have not been success-ful, they will be very demotivated indeed if a new person turns up before they know they have not got the job.

Company personnel

Once you have written to all unsuccessful applicants, the final step is to inform everyone in the company that the job has been filled and to provide a brief biography of the successful candidate. To illustrate this, here are the announcements for the two jobs mentioned earlier.

New Logistics Department Secretary

We are pleased to announce that KATE GREEN is to take over Jenny Smith's responsibilities as Departmental Secretary in Logistics. Kate will report directly to Mr Jones, Head of Logistics, and will be responsible for maintaining all the records, preparing movement orders, and handling all enquiries concerning documentation. Kate has been working as the dispatcher in our transport section for the last three years. We look forward to Kate taking up her new role and our thanks go to Jenny and we wish her luck in her new career.

In the case of the Sales Manager, the recruitment process has led to the appointment of an outsider.

Sales Manager – Northern Region

We are very pleased to announce that JANE BROWN will join the company on 1 June as our Sales Manager for the Northern Region. Jane will report to Barry Davis, the Sales Director, and will have a team of five people working with her. Before joining the company, Jane worked as the Liverpool Area Sales Manager for ABC Ltd and has considerable experience that will be of value to us. We wish Jane every success as she builds our business in the North. She and her team will be based in our Lancaster office.

With everyone now in the picture, you can focus on the next stage of developing people – introducing the new person to the job and arranging their training and development.

CHAPTER FOUR

Getting started

One of the most unnerving experiences a person can have is the first day in a new job. Even if the person has been recruited from within the company, the experience is still stressful. If the person is to settle in and become productive quickly, there are a number of actions that you need to carry out.

First impressions count

First impressions count for the new staff member and the people they will be working with. How efficiently you manage the introductory period will govern how the person views the company – it will also govern how quickly the person settles in.

Pre-start activities

While the new member is working out their notice or taking a holiday, you must make one final check that you have received responses to your request for references – this will include a reference from the last employer. You should also raise all the necessary documentation for the personnel file and this may require you to contact the previous employer and request the official tax forms that will allow you to establish the employee's new relationship.

On the practical side, you will need to ensure that the person's new manager is fully briefed and that arrangements have been made to provide the appropriate working environment. In labouring types of job this means ensuring that overalls and safety equipment are ready, that machinery and tools are available and that someone is allocated to oversee the first few days. In managerial or administrative positions arrangements should include desk, chair, telephone, computer, and so on. All this sounds totally routine but you will come across many stories of how people have started a new job without the necessary tools or equipment and have thus wasted considerable amounts of time waiting for these.

You will also need to ensure that any security processes are in place — the receptionist should be notified of the new person's arrival, security lists need updating so that the guards know that a new person is due, any electronic door passes need to be prepared so that they can be issued on the first day, and a car pass or parking space allocated. If a company car is to be part of the package then a vehicle must be allocated on a temporary basis until a new vehicle is chosen. You should also check that the person's new manager has prepared his briefing and decided on the work allocation.

First day: welcome

You should personally meet the new staff member when they first arrive and take them to your office so that any last-minute documentation can be dealt with. This is the time to issue company documentation and pass cards, and to answer any questions that the new person has. With this official part of the process over, and with the person in a reasonably relaxed state, you should arrange for the manager to come and collect his new team member.

How well the new person settles in is now down to the manager concerned — if they handle this right, then the team will meld very quickly but if it is handled badly it can take weeks before the new person settles in. To ensure things go well, the manager should use a checklist so that the whole day is thoroughly structured and the new team member is supervised at all times. (See Figure 4.1.)

At no time should the manager expect that the new person will undertake any productive work — this first day is

NEW ARRIVAL CHECKLIST

1 Official welcome away from the work
   location

2 Describe what will happen during the day

3 Establish that all central company matters
   have been completed

4 Escort the new team member to the work
   location

5 Show them where to hang coats and location
   of toilets, etc

6 Introduce each member of the team at their
   work locations

7 Brief on the current work of the department,
   the initial training programme, and first
   assignment

8 Show the team member their work location
   and ensure that all equipment is functioning,
   show them how to use the equipment, issue
   stationery and working clothes as necessary

9 Show them around the work location,
   including the safety routes and fire exits

10 Settle them at their work location and
   recommend that they spend time familiarising
   themselves with the equipment and
   documentation

11 Take them to lunch or arrange a team
   member to do so

12   Arrange that they meet with each team
      member on a one-to-one basis

13   Arrange for their inclusion on any
      communication lists and, if e-mail is used,
      that a welcome message is waiting

14   De-brief them at the end of the day

Fig. 4.1 Looking after the new recruit on day one

a time for familiarisation with the company, the team, the work, and the service departments and equipment. By establishing a tight structure for the day, the manager will ensure that the new team member will not have time to worry or feel uninvolved.

First week: supervision

During the first week, the manager needs to keep a close eye on the new team member and the work they are doing. Obviously the new person needs to be allocated work as soon as possible but the second day should start with a short meeting with the manager – new people are bound to have questions that have come to mind after their first day. Answering these questions is one of the most important things a manager can do to ensure that the person settles in – doing so demonstrates interest in the person.

The manager's close supervision of the first week's work needs to be positioned carefully so that the person feels neither under pressure nor singled out for attention. Figure 4.2 shows the level and tone of supervision which the manager should adopt.

At the end of the first week you should visit the new

PRELIMINARY SUPERVISION: WEEK ONE

1   Explain the process.

'During your first week I'll be spending quite a lot of time with you so that I can be sure that you're fully familiar with the work and to answer the questions you may have. Initially, I'll check with you on progress three or four times each day but by the end of the week I expect it'll be down to a couple of times. Of course, if you have any questions in the meantime, come and see me.'

2   Check at intervals.

Ask if they have any questions, check to see what they've done and whether it is up to standard, correct performance as necessary.

3   Review the day's work at the end of each day.

Meet with the person and review the work done. Check the standard and answer any questions. Allocate the next day's work.

Fig. 4.2 The new recruit's first week

team member at their work location to ensure that they have settled in and are happy with the way things are going. You should also talk to the manager to obtain feedback on the performance. This meeting is very important as the manager will have identified or confirmed any areas of skill weakness and can advise you on what skills training will be necessary.

First month: understanding the company

Before the end of the first month the new team member should attend an orientation seminar that explains in some detail the aims and objectives of the company, its mission statement, its policies and its structure. This seminar will probably take just one day for lower-level workers but a longer course may be necessary for managers.

Held away from the work environment, the seminar involves everyone who has joined in the last month – if that is only one person it doesn't matter, the orientation process should still take place. It is advisable that one or more of the senior managers are involved and the chief executive or managing director should talk about the mission statement. The objective of this is to involve the new people in the company and to obtain their commitment.

The mission statement is a single paragraph that encapsulates how the senior management thinks about the company. It must be precise, short enough to be remembered, realistic but challenging and must be written in simple and direct language:

> To be the supplier of choice to the automotive trade for quality-engineered widgets and to take a 20% market share by December ... (*year*) ...

or

> To be the market leader by ... (*year*) ... in the provision of customised software solutions to the offshore oil and gas exploration industry.

By involving the new staff in the seminar, you are pre-handling a number of issues that can and do arise because people do not understand how the company works. Explaining who does what, and where, often eliminates problems associated with inter-functional cooperation. Providing each person with the details of the company structure and of the principal managers gives them the feeling they are involved and are part of the company effort.

The orientation seminar should also address things like who to talk to about their work, about holidays and sick leave, about improving conditions, and all the many other things that staff want to know or can contribute towards. It should also provide details of the training programme that each person must go through, and explain the company's coaching and mentoring programme.

First three months: basic training

Even if you have been very lucky and the person you have recruited matches your specifications almost exactly, there will still be areas where the person's primary skills need to be enhanced if they are to deliver the standard of performance that the company requires. To address this you will need to establish a short training programme for the person.

This basic skills training course provides psychological benefits to the employee as well as enhanced performance. With early training, the person will start to produce higher-quality work and an enhanced performance sooner rather than later. The psychological benefits are that early training shows that the company is genuinely interested in 'investing in people', that it cares about its staff and that company performance is a high priority.

The basic skills training is a one-to-one course that has to be tailored specifically to the needs of the individual and it must focus on enhancing those skills that are weak. This is not a course to provide new skills over and above those required for the job – that comes later. It is specifically to address the mismatch between the person's skill level and that required to meet the job specification and performance standard. If the recruitment process has been carried out well, then this course is unlikely to take more than one or two days.

The course should be scheduled and delivered within three months of the person taking up the job; and successful completion of the course (and, consequently, delivering the right performance) will be prerequisites for the successful completion of the probationary period.

Any other performance-related problems or skill standards can be dealt with by the ongoing coaching programme and the manager should be noting carefully the additional areas where training could enhance the performance. It could be argued that all training should be done as soon as possible but you would be unwise to invest too much in training until the new team member has successfully passed the probationary period. If they do, then they become fully fledged members of the company and you will have had time to prepare a proper training programme interlinked to their future career development. If they fail the probationary period, then you will not have lost too much money and you will not have trained someone else's employee.

The probationary period

The probationary period is a trial period during which both the new employee and the company assess each other to see if they really are suited. It is not a one-sided contract: either side may terminate the employment relationship during the probationary period and give no reason. After the agreed period, normally six months, the contract between the two parties takes on a more solid nature and a long-term relationship is established.

You will need to make sure that everyone involved fully understands that this trial period is for the benefit of both parties and not used as a time to obtain cheap labour. The compensation package offered to the new employee is fully operational during the trial period but the pension contributions may be held uninvested until the period is over – at which point, you will either invest them in the pension scheme or hand them over to the employee if they or you decide to terminate the relationship.

Holiday entitlement

Many companies also impose a restriction on taking holidays during the probationary period. This is understandable and is unlikely to cause a problem unless the employee had booked a holiday before joining. In this case, as a good employer, you would almost certainly need to honour their booking and allow them their vacation. However, if no holiday is booked before joining, then normally no holiday entitlement is accrued until after the probationary period has been completed.

Standards of performance

Although you may be tempted to limit the exposure of the company during this time by not fully involving the new person, this is counter-productive and you should treat the person as a full employee from day one. The only thing you may choose to limit is the level of the performance-enhancing goals (see page 78). It will take the person a few months before they are fully 'up to speed' and, during this time, performance-enhancing goals should be kept to a minimum; however, the agreed Minimum Performance Standard (MPS) for the job will have to be achieved quickly.

Job title

If the company has corporate job titles such as Vice-President, Senior Manager, or whatever, there may be a policy to hold back on confirming the title during the trial period. This can seem petty, especially when the corporate title only impacts on the internal structure, and it can cause a considerable amount of friction. It would be reasonable to argue that if someone is doing a specific job then the title that goes with that job should be awarded immediately; the counter argument is that until the person has completed a trial period and proved they can do the job they should not receive all the corporate benefits. Unless you have linked benefits to the corporate title and not to the functional title this latter argument is hardly worth consideration when talking about titles.

Duration

In many countries, the probationary period is governed by law and protection against unfair dismissal, or dismissal for unspecified reasons, is not available to the employee until the period is over. This allows the company to make a fair assessment without the threat of legal action. You must, of course, obey the legal requirements but if the law requires a minimum probationary period of less than six months then you should have your employment contract drafted with a six-month period. It is unlikely that a proper assessment by either party can take place in a shorter period of time.

Regular 'health checks'

Throughout the first six months – the normal length of the probationary period – you should be meeting with the team member once a month and receiving development reports from the manager. This progress monitoring is to ensure that the new member is fitting in and settling down and that no unusual skill or performance deficiencies have shown up.

Monthly appraisals – both by the manager and the staff member – are vital and they should be formalised so that both parties are fully aware of how each views the work performance of the last month. There should be no surprises for either party and the appraisal should form the basis of the training-needs analysis that you will be carrying out for implementation after the probationary period.

The actual appraisals at this stage must be as objective as possible and a form should be used, listing the skills and providing a scale against which to judge performance. Obviously, this cannot be entirely objective but by carefully defining the skills and MPS it is possible to achieve a close approximation. Figure 4.3 illustrates such an appraisal form – although this is for a lathe operator, a similar form can be designed for any job as it is based directly on the job specifications.

Although the appraisal form may not record the MPS for each job, it does identify all the key requirements and implicitly refers to the specifications for the individual jobs. In addition, the form should consider attendance at

---

Probationary Appraisal

Name: *George SMITH*   Function: *Lathe operator*

Start Date: *1 May 1998*   Appraisal period: *August 1998*

Grading: 5 = Always   3 = Usually   1 = Hardly ever   0 = Never

- Establishes job requirements at outset.   5 4 3 2 1 0

- Sets up machine and machines a
  test piece within specifications.   5 4 3 2 1 0

- Machines all items within specifications with less
  than 5% error rate.   5 4 3 2 1 0

- Carries out random quality testing as required.   5 4 3 2 1 0

- Achieves specified run rate.   5 4 3 2 1 0

- Completes job sheets and submits them with
  the job.   5 4 3 2 1 0

- Carries out required and regular maintenance.   5 4 3 2 1 0

Fig. 4.3 An example of a monthly appraisal form

training courses, coaching sessions, time-keeping, cleanliness of the work environment and just about anything else that will help judge the person's effectiveness. Since the objective is to find out two things: (i) whether the skills are being delivered according to the required job MPS, and (ii) whether the person is fitting in with the team, the appraisal form must question both skills and desirable attributes. The acceptable minimum score for skills is likely to be 4 (nearly always) and for attributes, such as time-keeping, it should be at least 3 (usually). A score of 3 or below on skills indicates a developmental requirement that can either be addressed through coaching or training. A score of 2 or below on a desirable attribute would indicate the need for improvement that should be addressed through good management by the line manager, or a quiet word from you.

Your own meeting with the manager is to discuss developmental needs and to structure the coaching, whereas the meeting with the new staff member is to discuss both development needs and 'welfare' items. As the person settles in to the company, they will become curious about policies, employment conditions, future prospects and a thousand and one other items. Many of their questions are best handled by their manager but some are really in your domain and you must do your best to answer them.

After about five months you and the manager should meet to make the decision about confirming the employment contract. You may also decide to take soundings from other members of the team and those with whom the person has come in contact – suppliers, customers, and other departments. All this information needs correlating and placing in the personnel file. Towards the middle of the last month, you will meet the staff member to discuss their reactions and plan the way forward.

Assuming everything is positive then, as soon as the probationary period is over, you write to the new employee stating that the company wishes to confirm the appointment and asking them to write or sign a letter confirming that they, also, wish to continue.

Joining the full programme of human resources management

Once the probationary period has been completed, the new employee becomes eligible for all the benefits and conditions of employment within your company as specified in the terms and conditions section of the contract. But, at the same time, they also become subject to all the performance-management techniques and development processes that you have in operation.

Performance-enhancing goals (PEGs)

The new team member should now share in the team goals. Managers should revise performance to take into account the additional resource and then establish new performance-enhancing goals for everyone. This may present a psychological problem for the new person unless they have previously been in a 'goal' environment. Goal-setting is a private, one-to-one activity and, if done correctly, can overcome any psychological barriers.

Goals must conform to a specific structure if they are to be fully effective and this goes beyond just a *do what by when* structure.

Performance-enhancing goals can be set in all jobs although for many of the more administrative or routine labouring type activities it can seem difficult to set realistic goals – sometimes the MPS for the job is all that is wanted or needed in the way of performance. However, if the company is to grow then it needs everyone to perform to a higher standard. Many goals will be of the 'quality' type –

GOAL-SETTING MODEL

1   In a private interview, remind the person of their performance during the last goal period (month or quarter)

2   Ask them what they think they can achieve in the forthcoming period

3   Review this with the person to ensure that it is in line with expectations and ability in the current environment

4   Ensure that you and the team member believe the goal is possible

5   Agree the goal and *write it down*

answering telephones within three rings, handling problems or enquiries within one working day, fulfilling requests for parts within one hour, and so on. On the other hand, sales people can be targeted with sales volumes – either monetary or volume of goods. Everyone can and should have PEGs.

Because of the monthly appraisal system in place during the first six months, both the manager and the new team member know what the latter is capable of and the performance-enhancing goal should be the best monthly performance plus 10%. Care must be taken to ensure that the goal is met so that the person builds their self-confidence in their own ability to meet goals. This will involve the manager in taking an active interest in performance and they may even want to continue with monthly appraisals.

For the first three months after the probationary period, monthly goals should be used even if the company's policy

SMART GOAL STRUCTURE

1   **S**pecific: the goal must be very specific in what is to be achieved

2   **M**easurable: the result must be measurable or observable

3   **A**ccepted: both the manager and the employee must accept the goal parameters

4   **R**ealistic: the goal has to be achievable by that person, with their current level of ability, working in the existing market or environment

5   **T**imed: a fixed time must be allocated to a goal

is to use quarterly goals. Once the person has demonstrated their ability to meet a monthly PEG consistently, then they can be targeted with quarterly goals.

Feedback

Goals are motivational, enable the company to achieve growth, and help the individuals to develop, but they are only useful if both the manager and the person concerned have feedback of actual performance against the goal. This feedback must be accurate, continuously available, and readily understandable. Research shows that the best way to achieve this is to use a graphic representation of the goals with each person's performance recorded as a percentage of the individual goal.

It is quite common to come across feedback that is provided as a total volume (e.g. number of widgets made, number of widgets sold, monetary value of widgets sold) against a published goal. While there is nothing fundamentally wrong with this approach, it fails to deliver some of the most significant benefits associated with goals, and even sets up problems. The principal purpose of a goal is *to motivate the individual to deliver a superior performance* so that the company can obtain the benefit of that performance. Since it is an individual goal, the actual level of that goal is kept private between the manager and the team member. The person must be motivated to perform against the goal and not to compete against other team members who may be more experienced. Performance feedback must recognise this and the public display should not record each person's goal but merely their performance against the goal *in percentage terms*, since for the team to achieve its goal all members of the team must achieve their goals.

The process used to provide continuous feedback on performance will have to be explained and the new team member added to the charts. This will enable the person to see how their performance is progressing (in terms of percentage of goal) and will make them feel a part of the team. Feedback is, therefore, an important part of team-building as well as performance-monitoring.

Development – training, coaching and mentoring

After finding the right person to fill the right job, the second most important element of recruitment is to develop them so that there is a process of continuous improvement. In the ever more competitive world of business, no company can afford not to improve its performance and improved performance comes from people producing more, to a higher standard, quicker, more efficiently and with greater flexibility. All these things are possible if people are developed and managed in the right way.

The process of development is based on *training* people in new or advanced skills, then *coaching* those skills until they are second-nature. Whenever performance declines, for whatever reason, *coaching* is used to address the issue. Developing the career of each person in the company to the greatest advantage of the company and the person concerned is then handled by *mentoring*. These three areas – training, coaching and mentoring – are discussed in Parts Two and Three.

Finally, people need to be managed in the right way. There is a whole range of performance-management techniques that have to be used and Part Three focuses on those that are implemented by the company rather than by the individual managers. They include team-management, motivation, performance appraisals, recognition and reward of performance and career advancement through change or promotion.

PART TWO: TRAINING & COACHING

Ensuring the right skills are used in the right way

While you will have made every effort to ensure that you have recruited only those people who have the right skills – the skills that will enable them to do the job you want to the standard you require – nobody is perfect and new staff, as well as existing staff, will need developing through training and coaching.

Training and coaching are interdependent – *training* is the formal teaching of skills while *coaching* is the process you use to implement the training and to ensure that the skills continue to be used in the right way in the work environment. Coaching alone can never replace the formal training programme and both are a major investment in the development of top-quality staff.

Training is, without a doubt, a strategic activity and yet the following scenario happens all the time: performance starts to fade, the market place becomes that much tougher to operate in, senior management looks for ways to reduce costs and, wham, the training budget is slashed and managers are expected to coach their teams more to compensate.

Why do companies do this? The answer is a lack of understanding of the role training plays in the development of the business and a failure to grasp the fact that training and coaching are not the same thing.

It is worth repeating that training is the formal teaching of skills whereas coaching is the process of ensuring those skills are properly used. Training is a strategic activity whereas coaching is a tactical tool.

In the following three chapters we will be looking at:

■   Training and setting up a training programme

■   Coaching – the implementation of training

■   Setting up a coaching programme

CHAPTER FIVE

Training – the basis of development

The training philosophy

Training is the basis for the development of people and the first thing you have to decide is to what extent you are going to develop your staff.

There is a recognisable philosophy in many companies that skills can be 'bought' by recruiting the right people and that if higher-level skills are required then a new person will be recruited and the previous incumbent 'released to pursue their career elsewhere'. This does work – up to a point. The problem is that all the Human Resources budget will be focused on recruitment because of the high turnover of staff as ever-increasing skills are required. In addition, other staff see this turnover and feel insecure and they start leaving. After a while, if only a few experienced managers are left and the rest of the staff are very new, this ultimately leads to declining performance, a drop in profitability, and a general collapse of the company's fortunes.

A wise company, on the other hand, will certainly try to recruit the right people *but it will then develop them so that improved skills lead to improved performance*. The Human Resources budget is better spent in developing quality staff through investment in training than through constant recruitment. If the investment is in development then an investment return can be generated to the overall benefit of the organisation.

But this requires that a training philosophy is consciously developed using the strategic model shown, which looks at

STRATEGIC TRAINING MODEL

1   Basic education is assumed – no one is recruited without it

2   Each functional job requires core skills and knowledge which are identified and recorded in the job description

3   Core skills and basic knowledge appropriate to a function are assumed – no one is recruited without them

4   Training in basic functional skills is available to address deficiencies

5   Orientation training has to be provided

6   A training matrix exists for all functional jobs

7   Career development is dependent on completing the prescribed training as well as performance and other selection criteria

the key issues that need to be considered.

There is one basic concept that underpins this approach: the management of human resources – of people – within the company is aimed at fulfilling the strategic objectives of the organisation. This is the same concept that underpins the recruitment process discussed in Part One. If you have a clear strategic objective you can plan what resources you need to achieve the objective. As the objectives change and grow, resources also need to change and grow and this applies to people as much as to anything else. Some may argue that to regard people in this way is demeaning and wrong but the fact remains that it is a matter of reality – you employ people to fulfil a business requirement and not as a social service.

In the model above the first three items are essentially self-explanatory – the recruitment process should ensure that all employees have a basic education (some will need further education); the job description identifies the main functional skills and knowledge required; and you will not have taken on anyone who does not have them. The fourth item – training in basic skills to address deficiencies – may seem a contradiction (after all, you will have recruited someone with the right skills), but the truth is that no one has all the skills we need and some additional training will be needed.

Addressing skills deficiencies

When a new member of the team is first brought in, their performance will almost certainly be below that which they are capable of producing. This is a result of the fact that each job, no matter how similar it may seem to another, is subtly different – slightly different equipment, slightly different materials, differences in management style, a different way of doing things – and the new person will have to adjust their skills accordingly. In many areas the adjustment is small and quickly learned on the job, but in others the person's skills may be rusty from lack of use, or different skills are needed. The deficiency is *specific to the job and to the person*, so the training needs to be as well. But person-specific training requires a great deal of flexibility in the training programme and you must consciously build this in.

Orientation training

This process was discussed in chapter four. Unlike training in skills, it is not job- or person-specific and you should develop a corporate orientation seminar for use with all new members of staff, irrespective of their function. By having a common programme you ensure that everyone has the same basic knowledge about the company and how it operates. They know what it stands for, what it does, how it is organised, who the principal managers are, and what overall objectives have to be achieved. As mentioned earlier, this seminar must include the company's mission statement or vision and senior managers must help in the delivery so that new staff are made to feel part of the corporate team.

Philosophically, the cultural or orientation programme is there as a team-building device that aims to obtain commitment *from* new staff at an early stage by showing commitment *to* them. No one likes to feel that all they are is a cog in a giant and impersonal machine; they want to feel important, even if they are only a cog, and the quickest way to achieve this is to involve them in a corporate-culture seminar.

In addition, the seminar must stress that everyone needs to produce 100% of their goals if the company is to achieve its goals, and if the company is successful then everyone will be recognised and rewarded in some way.

The training matrix

The training matrix details who should undertake what training at what stage of their career. It is central to the training philosophy and determines the overall design of the training programme. It is a strategic document and, as such, is the responsibility of the senior management team or, if there is one, the senior Human Resources manager.

The training matrix should be updated regularly to ensure that the objective of the programme supports the overall objectives of the company. In addition, it must also be kept current so that you know at any time the state of training and development of each and every individual in the company.

The starting point for the matrix is to record, from the job description, the skills that are *prerequisites* and those that are *desirable* for each and every job. Although core functional skills are assumed as a result of the recruitment process, the programme should contain courses to improve them and to provide advanced skills, with the overall objective of ensuring that each person has the skills necessary to meet ever more demanding performance goals.

Obviously, there are some jobs in which all the functional skills are prerequisites – machinists, assembly and process workers, computer operators, to name a few – and the only training these people are likely to receive is a single course designed to enhance existing skills or an equipment-specific session to handle a new machine or piece of equipment. On the other hand, these same people may display aptitudes that, with training, would allow them to undertake a different job in the future and you might slot them into a different programme.

In contrast, there are many jobs, often in junior and middle management, that require a constantly improving set of skills, along with additional knowledge. These jobs will have a more comprehensive training programme that develops these people along a specific path and in a specific manner. Such jobs require regular training commitments and you may like to build into the job description the fact that the person will be required to undertake a specified number of days' training each year.

Training is an essential part of career development

You will also need a coherent approach to people's career development and career opportunities should only be made available if the person has completed the necessary steps in the training matrix. However, the company is not there to act as a training centre and, more controversially, it is not there to provide training and development that does not contribute directly to the commercial objectives that have to be achieved. Whilst development should be encouraged, it must also be focused: providing language training for a lathe operator at the company's expense is only valid if they will then take up a job in which those new skills will have a place.

Training is not a reward. Some employers try to use participation in training as a reward for performance. This is to fundamentally misunderstand the purpose of training – you reward performance through recognition, enhanced benefits or a bonus scheme, but you train as a strategic activity for the development of the company. To use it in any other way is to trivialise it and to downgrade its importance.

Training is not optional. There are plenty of companies around whose management regard the training schemes as optional – they put their people on the course and then take them off if some requirement arises. This is demotivating to the employee and a reflection of bad management. There are even managers who are so convinced that they are indispensable that, when they are told to attend training, they simply ignore the instruction and fail to turn up. Undoubtedly they will come up with creative excuses, some of which will sound plausible, but managers who approach training this way are the ones most in need of it and are probably the least effective. If training is required, then those who are to undergo the training must attend.

Internal or external training provision?

Perhaps the biggest problem you will face is whether to supply the training using internal or external resources. There are pros and cons to each and you must examine these with care. In general, beyond the orientation seminar and any other training courses that are of necessity internal, the training programme can be provided by external training resources or by internal ones – the primary deciding factor being one of budget.

If your company is a small- to medium-sized enterprise with up to 500 employees it is unlikely that the internal provision of the whole training programme will be economically viable. Of course, there will be a number of training courses that you can provide internally but unless you have someone dedicated to training then this will prove difficult.

The professional approach

Training is not something that can be delivered by just anyone – to be effective it needs people who themselves have had professional training in the delivery of educational material and experience in the types of courses you require. Such a professional team can and should be supplemented by senior staff who are designated to deliver specific modules.

It is possible that, if your company is large enough, you will have training staff. If this is not the case then you will need to establish a group of professional trainers that you can call on. These people are generally freelance independents who can work with just about any material. Each will have specialisations but most are competent in a variety of training areas. Finding such people is never a straightforward activity and you may need to make enquiries with the Human Resources managers of major companies or with the main training organisations.

As with recruiting anybody, you will need to interview the trainers and see them in action by attending one of their seminars or watching a video of them at work. You will also need to be certain about what you expect them to do (develop material, deliver material) and how much they expect to be paid. Being consultants, they will have a fee structure based on preparation and training days and will invoice accordingly.

You should be wise to take the time to get to know the

available trainers and their styles whether you are planning on internal or external provision.

Internal provision

The benefits of internal provision are that you are much more in control of the content, the style of presentation, the costs and the follow-up process. This level of control has led many companies to feel that internal provision is the best approach, but there are a number of disadvantages. The capital investment in training facilities and the ongoing costs of employing training staff often outweigh the benefits. Additionally, unless you are employing training professionals, the development of course material is time-consuming (and thus expensive) and often requires a considerable amount of research.

External provision

The cost of maintaining an internal training unit has led more and more companies to using external training providers. And, in general, they have turned to commercial training companies hoping that 'off-the-shelf' courses will meet their requirements. They might. Equally, they might not and care must be taken in the selection of provider and what they are offering in terms of course and content. Fortunately, most commercial training companies have realised that each and every customer is different and, although much material is common, large amounts have to be prepared specially.

But external provision can be highly cost-effective and need not be confined to the use of commercial training organisations. Much of your training requirement will be for skills courses for the lower end of the workforce – machinists, secretaries, assembly workers, technicians, computer operators, stores personnel, drivers, administrative assistants, and so on. Most, if not all, of these can attend training courses developed and run by technical colleges,

NVQ (National Vocational Qualification) training organisations, specialist training units and a number of other public-sector educational institutions. In almost all cases, certification is by examination and the successful trainee thereby achieves an additional qualification that is recognised nationally. Almost all these courses can be carried out full time, part time, or on specified evenings, and many institutions are willing to set up company-specific courses if the numbers attending are high enough.

A similar pattern of provision is also available for junior and middle management people. There are commercial providers and, again, courses are available at institutions ranging from the local technical college through professional training centres to management colleges and universities.

The real benefit of the public-sector approach is that training can be provided for small numbers spread across a wide range of courses and you do not have the problem of getting an adequate number of people to attend a company-specific course. This means that training can generally be provided at the right level at the right time to suit each individual member of the company's staff. The other significant benefit is that course fees tend to be much lower in the public-sector institutions than they are in the commercial training companies.

The downside is that course content is frequently outside your control and the skills and knowledge are generally presented in generic terms. For most training requirements this is unlikely to be a problem as the implementation of the new skills in the work environment can be handled through coaching. However, to minimise this apparent disadvantage you should select the course carefully, basing your decisions both on the prospectus and on a visit to the training facilities to meet the instructors.

Structure of training courses

Whether you use internal or external providers for the majority of the training, you will still need to run a number of internal courses – the orientation seminar, corporate culture and open-book seminars, training sessions relating to new procedures or equipment, and courses that cannot be provided in the normal way either because of small group-size or lack of availability through your normal provider. In these cases, you will need to develop your own course material and structure the training sessions to get the best from the event.

The principal structure of a training session can be summarised as follows:

- Tell them what you are going to tell them
- Tell them
- Tell them what you've told them
- Practise, practise, practise

Tell them what you are going to tell them

The training sessions will need to be structured carefully so that they build logically on each other. As this is done, the trainer will identify the objectives of each session, and these will provide the core from which to develop the material. However, if the learning experience is to be effective, it is insufficient that only the course leader or programme director knows what has to be achieved in each session. If you are not to waste time, the trainees also need to know and understand what has to be achieved. Hiding the objective, disguising it, or allowing it to be a surprise revealed during the session results in diminished effectiveness of the training and a strong likelihood that the information and training will not be retained.

Therefore, the first, and most important, step is to set out the objectives of the session before work commences. This means explaining exactly:

■ what is going to be covered

■ what they should understand and learn from it (the learning objectives).

Establishing the learning objectives at the start helps to focus the mind of the trainees on what is to be discussed and learned. It also acts as a signpost for them during the session and it keeps the trainer on track.

A good approach is to put up an overhead slide with the session's objectives clearly stated – for example, Figure 5.1 shows the opening slide for a training session on how to sell.

Sales model

Objective
• To develop a model for a sales interview

Session outcome
• To understand the model and its applicability

• To be able to apply the model

• To demonstrate both theoretical and practical understanding of the model

• To demonstrate the ability to use the model via practical role-plays.

Fig. 5.1 Training session opener: what you will be doing

Tell them

This is the main body of the training session and will cover all the material to achieve the objective and to allow the trainees to reach the desired outcome. Clearly, therefore, this part must be structured so that it builds logically towards the objectives while allowing adequate time for them to demonstrate (i) their understanding of the material and (ii) that they can apply the new skill in a practical manner.

Tell them what you've told them

Again, the use of overhead slides to put up the summary of the session focuses everyone's attention. All the key points should be clearly identified in the order they were made and all linkages should be obvious. The trainer should also hand out a summary sheet or detailed notes so that the trainees have the facts in an easy-to-understand format that covers everything.

Practise, practise, practise

In addition to the short practice opportunities within the main body of the session, once the theoretical side has been covered, plenty of time should be devoted to the practice of the skill through a wide variety of role-plays. The time to practise the skill is in the training session and not in the workplace. If people re-enter the workplace having practised their new skills then they are less likely to make mistakes and thus incur costs to the company or require additional training or coaching.

This structure can also be used when providing people with the opportunity to acquire knowledge – it is not just confined to skills training. Structured learning helps place the knowledge in perspective and aids acquisition, providing that the knowledge is given out in a logical and progressive manner.

Self-directed training

A great deal has been made of self-directed training as if, by making the individual responsible for their own training, the company can save on training fees. This may well be true, but in the long run the savings may not be extensive. Setting up a self-directed programme requires the same care and attention as setting up a more traditional programme. As with all training, self-directed training requires analysis of the training requirements of the company to determine what needs to be taught and to whom. Once this has been done, a selection process has to be implemented to identify what training can actually be handled by the self-directed method – then, and only then, can the programme be developed.

There is a range of self-directed training programmes available and these include:

- paper-based

- audio- and video cassette-based

- computer-based with interactive dedicated software

- CD-ROM-based interactive programmes

- distance learning

- virtual training.

Self-directed training programmes are generally multimedia-based with a strong emphasis on the use of interactive computer programmes. Early examples of such programmes relied heavily on audio tapes and later combined these with videos – a typical example is the language course in which the student listens to the tape and repeats the sounds and tries to understand what is being said. To assist them they also have a detailed course book which occasionally requires written work. With the advent

97

of widely available PCs with CD-ROM drives, the focus has moved to interactive programmes that often include sound as well as text and graphics.

Such programmes are neither easy to construct nor are they cheap, and, unless there is a mass market, they tend to be an impractical solution for a small company to develop. This has led to a divergence within this type of training – generic programmes have been developed on CD-ROM and specific programmes have been developed to work on dedicated systems.

CD-ROM-based generic programmes have the advantage that they are cheap to buy but have the significant disadvantage that they do not – cannot – address the specific requirements of an individual company. However, where generic skills are being sought – as for sales, telephone techniques, etc. – they are a very valuable resource.

Specialised programmes for dedicated systems are obviously far more expensive as they involve hardware (the dedicated computers) and a good deal of programming. However, where the main focus of the training is the imparting of knowledge rather than skills, this too is a valuable resource.

The main advantage of all self-directed training programmes is that individuals can receive training as and when it suits their workload and changing job requirements without the need for a course to be set up.

The main disadvantages are, however, significant in *training* terms. For example:

■ Different individuals have different learning styles and the programme may not be appropriate.

■ Different individuals have different levels of motivation and may not have the discipline necessary.

■ All trainees have questions during their training – in normal circumstances these would be addressed to the trainer so that the absence of the trainer is likely to diminish the value of the training.

■ Not everybody understands things in the same way – a skilled trainer overcomes this problem by presenting the information in a variety of ways. In a self-directed programme the trainees may skip the bits they find difficult.

■ Finally, whereas conventional training generally results in the individual having a firm grasp of the new skills and knowledge and being able to put them into practice *because the trainer has ensured they can*, the self-directed programme puts far more emphasis on the need for coaching in the work environment, and in real situations, to ensure the skills are used. This transfers the training/coaching from the experienced trainer to the line manager who may well have too little time, no inclination, and insufficient skills in this field.

In general, therefore, self-directed programmes are very useful for the teaching of knowledge but are less effective for the teaching of skills, and have significant disadvantages in training terms. Measuring their true effectiveness and the investment return is, in consequence, more difficult.

Distance learning

The latest advances in self-directed learning have combined the best of the CD-ROM and computer materials with access to trainers via e-mail and fax. The origin of this approach was the correspondence course which flourished during the 1950s and '60s. The problem, however, was the slowness of the process – submitting work or questions by post, the time taken for the tutor to reply, and then waiting for the postal system to deliver the letter, made the whole thing very time-consuming and inefficient in learning terms. This has now been overcome through the use of the Internet and e-mail for rapid communications.

The speed of response is now limited only by how fast the tutor can respond to the students' questions. The ease with which material can be handled electronically means that the constraints of correspondence courses no longer apply – for example: essays and projects can be submitted and assessed, feedback can be given, and the item amended, edited and resubmitted without the need for time-consuming rewriting and retyping. Tutors can almost establish a dialogue while on-line, with answers taking just minutes to arrive and, with the development of 'chat' software, direct discussion (via the keyboard and screen) can take place between individuals or even with groups. The development of the Internet and its associated software has allowed trainees to become involved with learning without the need to travel to the training location.

Distance learning is, however, not the answer to all training needs. Like all self-directed learning, it suffers limitations, not the least of which is the need for a great deal of self-discipline from the trainee. And, of course, using this method you cannot train a person in practical skills such as how to use a lathe or drive a fork-lift truck.

Virtual training

The advances in programming techniques and superfast 'chips' have allowed the development of 'virtual reality' software for which the operator wears a helmet and special gloves that are connected to the computer. The helmet allows the person to 'see', and the gloves allow them to 'operate', machinery and equipment that is programmed into the computer. In this way, the operator can carry out thousands of actions in a 'real' environment without moving away from the computer.

The well-known examples of this sort of technology include the flight simulators used to train pilots (not true 'virtual reality' but getting that way), and the latest training equipment for tank crews who can now practise without cost, and the ever more complex games arcade equipment found in almost all big towns.

Taking this concept and putting it into a training environment means that people can be trained to operate machinery, drive fork-lift trucks, assemble products, and carry out almost all other functional skills including interpersonal and customer-contact skills without risk, without cost and over and over again, all without leaving the computer. Skills training could be transformed within a short while through the use of 'virtual reality' and this is an area to watch.

Measuring the investment return on training

Training people is expensive. It is, however, an investment and, like all investments, it must provide a measurable return. But does this mean it has to provide a *financial* return? Some training has a direct impact on profitability and thus the financial return is measurable. The cost of the training is measurable – seminar leader fees, delegate fees, hotel and food, temporary cover where necessary – and this represents the investment. The net increase in productivity, as measured by the increase in revenues or reduction in costs, can be recorded. The increase in productivity is the investment return on training and the financial return is the increase in revenues/reduction in costs less the cost of training.

This illustrates a number of key factors involved in the measurement of the value of training: the exact cost of the training must be calculated both in terms of the overall programme and in terms of the number of participants; the area of expected impact of the training and a predetermined method of measuring it must be agreed before the training commences; external factors need to be taken into account; and a starting point determined. This last point is vital — very few operations have a zero starting point and knowing the revenue at the start allows the difference to be calculated. In commercial terms, it is the difference in performance that determines the value of the training.

Measuring the effectiveness of training

There is more to measuring training than calculating its financial return. All measurements require a benchmark at the start and a differential at the end. Some measurements are self-evident — take riding a bicycle: at the beginning of the training the person cannot ride a bicycle — they cannot mount it, balance on it, move it, steer it, or stop it. At the end of the training they can do all those things. It is not necessary to carry out a formal appraisal process to see if the training was effective.

Another form of one-off evaluation is the formal examination. This can be either by observation, as with riding a bicycle, or in a written format. The first approach is suitable for practical skills while the latter is often the most effective way of ensuring knowledge has been learned. You might like to consider the use of formal qualifications as part of the training programme. Everyone who attends training likes to have a certification that 'proves' (a) they have undertaken the training, and (b) they have reached a predefined standard. Various organisations exist to assist in the examination and certification process: the examining boards for academic qualifications (in England and Wales, GCSEs); and the NVQ

(National Vocational Qualification) and City & Guilds boards for practical skills. Even management and administrative skills can be examined and certified through professional institutes such as Institute of Chartered Accountants, Institute of Management and Institute of Directors, or through special arrangements with management colleges. Encouraging people to obtain recognised qualifications is both motivational and a useful way of tracking development.

Unfortunately, many training courses have no formal (or even informal) examination of any kind and the participant may not even be awarded a participation certificate. These courses, often of great value, have their impact lessened by the trainers not establishing that a certain 'formal' level of performance is required. To avoid this becoming a problem, or the courses being regarded as just a pleasant way of spending a few days, you should actively seek some sort of linkage with nationally recognised certification.

However, one-off observation or certification is insufficient. Having taught the skills, you then need to ensure that the person delivers those skills at a satisfactory level for a long period of time. In this case, it is necessary to establish what is 'a satisfactory level' and what is 'a long period of time'. Once these have been determined *they must be conveyed to the trainee at the beginning of their training* so that they understand the way they will be judged in the future. They should also be told what ongoing support they will receive to ensure the continued performance of the skills at an acceptable level.

This, of course, is where *coaching* comes into its own as a developmental tool.

CHAPTER SIX

Coaching – the implementation of training

As discussed in chapter five, training is a formal activity that takes place away from the work environment in a designated training area. The people who lead the training are 'trainers' – either specially trained staff skilled in teaching or line managers spending time in the training function. The training programme is formally structured and each course has a formal and logical format. On the other hand, the activity that many managers refer to as 'on-the-job training' is, in fact, not training at all and should be referred to as coaching. And the purpose of coaching is to implement the training the person has received, to embed it in the person's working practice and to ensure the skills are used at a consistently high standard.

Coaching is an activity that most employees place high on their list of desirable management or corporate practices. A recent staff survey for an international bank showed that those people who received regular and frequent coaching recorded significantly higher satisfaction with the corporation than those who received little or very infrequent coaching.

Not everyone in a company is well situated, or well suited, to take on the role of coach. Exactly who should be given this responsibility, and in what circumstances, is discussed in chapter seven. **The remainder of this chapter is addressed directly to the reader who has taken on responsibility for coaching others.** The coaching activity must, of course, be understood by the line manager, or team leader, even when someone else is carrying out the coaching.

What is coaching?

The philosophy of the coaching programme is best understood through consideration of the role of the coach.

The unbiased observer

First and foremost, the coach has to be an unbiased observer. They must be solely concerned with the correct and appropriate application of skills and be unconcerned with the general functioning of the team itself. Coaching is, therefore, a developmental and not a management activity.

The responsibility for the team's performance belongs to the team leader or manager, whereas the responsibility for the individual's performance belongs to the coach. Team leaders have a lot to do in achieving the team goals and objectives and it is not part of their role to *deliver* coaching – it is part of their role, however, to *ensure the coaching is delivered*. This is an important distinction and one that is seldom drawn in today's lean and delayered organisations – most of which expect the team leader or manager to act as coach as well as undertaking all their other responsibilities.

The team leader – the manager – is not an unbiased observer. They cannot afford poor performance by any member to affect the team. The team must perform as a whole if its objectives are to be achieved – and it is the direct responsibility of the leader to ensure that the team's objectives are achieved. Nor can today's team leader be an expert in all aspects of all the skills of all their team – today's teams are made up of people with wide-ranging skills and responsibilities.

Enter the coach – the unbiased observer of people's

performance. As coach, you are the person responsible for ensuring that each person is delivering their skills appropriately and to a consistently high standard. The team leader, when a decline in performance is observed, should first check if it is a motivational problem (that *is* the leader's responsibility) and, if it is not, then you call in the coach to spend time with the individual concerned.

Correcting skills

Obviously, a coach needs to fully understand the team member's skills and their correct application, but you do not have to be an expert in the skill. Many of the best coaches have only average competence in the application of the skills but, providing they know exactly how it is supposed to work, then they will be able to coach. This might seem strange, but the truth is that very few people can be truly expert in all the skills of any job – let alone of all the jobs involved in a team. Competence in and a full understanding of the role and the skills involved, combined with well-developed coaching skills is the key to successful coaching.

To coach a person and to correct their application of the skills, it is first necessary to observe the person in action and to analyse what they are doing and to compare this to what they should be doing – in this way what they are doing incorrectly or less effectively can be identified. This is not just a matter of watching for a few minutes, it is more likely to involve you in spending a day with the person as an observer. Accurate identification of problem areas cuts down the amount of time necessary to correct the overall performance.

The time spent on being coached is not necessarily time well spent as far as the recipient is concerned. However, most people wish to be more productive and more effective and thus if coaching *adds value* by being effective and focused (and does not waste time) then the person will not begrudge it and will even express greater satisfaction with their management if such coaching is made available on a regular and frequent basis.

Having identified the *problem*, you can then devise the best approach to correct the skills and to improve the performance. This will also require care to ensure that in correcting part of the performance another part is not made to suffer. The correct linkage between skills is vital.

Having determined the *approach*, you can then offer either:

■ corrective feedback in the workplace

or

■ pull the person out and coach in a non-work environment, or even offer one-to-one training.

The important thing to keep in mind is that when coaching, you are there to correct an inappropriately or incorrectly applied skill – not to retrain someone. If the incorrect application of the skills involved is too great then the person will need to be retrained in a training environment or on a training course. Remember, coaching and training are not the same thing; but they are complementary.

Corrective feedback

Many short-term performance problems arise from simple and often small errors in the way the skills are applied and, if these are addressed quickly, performance can be enhanced without the need for extensive coaching. Once identified, these types of problems can be addressed through the coaching skill of corrective feedback.

Corrective feedback is given as soon as the error is observed and is delivered informally. It can only be used for very simple errors as there is no time for the coach to spend in observation and preparation of a coaching plan.

CORRECTIVE FEEDBACK MODEL

1   Specify what was good about the observed performance

2   Specify what should be changed in the way the actions were carried out and how this can be done

3   Express confidence in the person and their ability to deliver the expected performance

Used correctly, corrective feedback leaves the person feeling good about themself but aware of the need to improve their performance. It enhances performance and is motivational – in time, it becomes welcome.

Coaching more complex skills or knowledge

Corrective feedback, if delivered immediately, is a highly successful way of addressing simple errors, but when wider issues, such as complex skills or a lack of knowledge, need to be addressed then you will need to establish a subject-specific coaching session.

A coaching session should be properly structured for maximum effect and the following five-step approach is a good model to follow.

1 Explain the purpose of the session

The first thing to do is arrange with the individual to meet you on a one-to-one basis – this should be done following an observation period. You must give them a positive view of the meeting otherwise they may develop resistance to the coaching. For example, you might say, 'Sue, having watched you doing the analysis of information acquisition and needs, I can see that there may be ways we could improve its efficiency. I'd like you to meet me in ... (*specify location, time and day*) ... so that we can work on it.' This structure shows that a weakness has been identified and that the meeting is to address that issue *together*.

When the person arrives, you should restate the purpose of the session in terms of the current performance versus the desired performance. For example, 'Sue, as agreed, we're going to be looking at the information-acquisition-and-needs-anaylsis part of the sale process. At the moment you seem to be doing it ... (*describe accurately what she is doing*) ... whereas the way it should be done is ... (*describe the desired approach*) ... Let's work on this to see how you can improve the effectiveness of what you're doing.'

2 Jointly examine the current situation

It is probable that the individual will not see their performance in the same way as you have just described it. They may also be defensive and this has to be overcome before the coaching will be of benefit. Spending time to reach an agreement on what they *are* doing in comparison to what they *should be* doing will save effort later.

You will have to use good probing skills with a lot of open-ended questions to get the individual to tell you what they consider to be the problem. And then spend time clarifying your understanding and ensuring that the two of you are in agreement over the situation. This will require guiding the person towards a fuller understanding of what they are doing and how it differs from the desired approach and how carrying out the skill correctly will enhance their performance.

During this process you are seeking the individual's agreement that their performance needs to be changed. This is a very important point since the coaching will only be successful if the person sees a need to change.

3 Working together, examine the possible coaching solutions

Having reached an agreement of what needs to be developed, you should (a) encourage the individual to tell you what they think should be done in terms of coaching, and (b) offer alternative solutions that may be more appropriate. The most effective change will occur when the individual identifies and proposes the solution for themself – they will be far more committed to their own plan than they will be to yours. The skill you will need is to ensure that the individual's plan is close to, or the same as, yours.

Once both parties have identified the best solution, you should reconfirm the individual's agreement to the course of action. For example, 'OK, Sue. We've agreed that the way you were carrying out the information-acquisition-and-needs analysis can be improved and that this will be done through me providing a coaching session following each of your next four sales calls. Are we OK so far?'

4 Implement the action plan

It is possible that the best solution will be for further training, in which case this can be scheduled. However, if the individual is a reasonably experienced member of the team then most developmental needs can be dealt with through coaching.

Whether you coach immediately or wait until a later point in time, you should use the following model.

- *Position the skill*
  Outline the whole of the process into which
  the skill fits and explain at exactly what point
  in the process the skills should be used.

- *Establish the relationship between the skill
  and the overall process*
  Identify the skill and how it works in relation
  to the rest of the process. If it is a multi-part
  skill then explain each part.

- *Provide examples of the skill in use*
  Take real examples of the skill in use and
  then role-play them so that the individual
  understands what is being done and has a
  model for doing it themself.

- *Practise the skill*
  It is very important at this stage that the
  individual attempts to use the skill – but,
  rather than letting them do this in a situation
  where failure will damage their confidence,
  got them to role-play the skill with you until
  they are 'word perfect'.

- *Practise the process*
  At this stage you should set up a role-play
  that involves the whole process. This allows
  you to check that the individual has absorbed
  the skill and can put it into the process
  effectively.
  Repeat the last two steps until you are
  satisfied the skill has been acquired and will
  be delivered to the desired performance
  standard.

5 Conclusion and follow-up

With the need to deliver a skill in a new way, it is likely that the individual will be slightly less confident than normal. You *must*, therefore, express your confidence in the individual's ability to use the skill correctly. This can be helped by establishing the follow-up process:

- you will be observing the person for a while to ensure the skill is being used correctly and to assist (through corrective feedback) whenever necessary

and

- you will repeat the coaching as often as necessary until the individual is entirely happy and confident with the skill.

It is very important to establish *and implement* the follow-up process as it does two things that are vital to the success of any coaching:

(i)   it tells the individual that an improvement in their performance is expected and that the correct use of skills is part of the Minimum Performance Standard for the job

and

(ii)   it ensures that any reversion to unacceptable performance is picked up very quickly and recoached. This reinforces the message that you are continuously monitoring performance and that development work is not a one-off event.

Coaching to develop performance

Although the primary purpose of coaching is to implement training or to correct an observed misuse of a skill, it should also be used as part of the development of each person's performance in their job. This goes beyond the correction or enhancement of specific skills and becomes a method for ensuring that everyone is performing at or above their Minimum Performance Standard. The responsibility for this sort of coaching is rarely often given to an 'unbiased observer' but to an individual's direct team leader. Team leaders would be unwise to wait until performance starts to decline before taking action, therefore they should schedule time with each person in their team to spend a 'typical' day with them. Sometimes called 'field-training', this type of coaching should occur on a regular basis – perhaps once a month with someone new to a position, perhaps once a quarter with someone who is experienced in the role – and everyone should be involved.

Team leaders, when responsible for coaching, must take care not to confuse a field-training day with the times that they spend with their people as part of their work. Whenever you are involved in the work process in any way, then that is not a good time to be offering coaching.

A field-training day needs careful preparation by both coach and individual, especially when customers are involved, and the following structure helps ensure that the time involved is well spent.

Step one – advance preparation

Confirm with your team member, at least one week in advance, that the scheduled field-training day is to take place and ask them to make sure that arrangements for the day are as normal as possible. The objective is to observe them going about their usual day-to-day activity but it is

113

also to watch them deliver all the skills involved in their work. It is absolutely no use spending a field-training day with a person unless they are involved in their normal work; if you suspect that the individual has set up the day to be easy and to show them in the best light, then you need to take corrective action.

A day or so before the field-training is due to take place, you and the individual should review the proposed programme to check that:

a) the individual has prepared the day properly with an adequate number of activities or meetings and sufficient time to provide feedback after each one

and

b) you understand what is going to happen during the day. This is very important – you need to concentrate on the coaching and any surprise alterations to the programme are a distraction.

Step two – pre-activity briefing

At the beginning of the day and before each activity, you should review the team member's preparation for that activity – especially if it involves clients.

You should check the aim of the meeting or activity – why is it taking place, what are its objectives, what is the expected, versus the desired, outcome?

If a client is involved – for example, a sales or service meeting – you should also review:

■ the client information – what is known about the client

■ the anticipated needs of the client or the opportunities that are being looked for

■ the expected attitude of the client towards the meeting, and any proposal that is to be put forward.

At this point you should also make it clear to your team member that they are in charge and that you are only an observer. You should also agree how you will be introduced to the client to ensure acceptance of your presence.

Step three – observation, the core of the coaching activity

With many activities it is possible just to observe the person carrying out their normal work. You know what has to be done and how the skills are supposed to be delivered and simple observation and note-taking may be all that is required. The situation becomes more complicated, however, when clients are involved in a face-to-face meeting.

You should allow the team member to introduce you and to explain why you are there. You should mention to the client (or others involved in the meeting) that you will be taking notes in your role as an observer. Then you need to keep unobtrusively in the background and out of eye contact with either the client or the team member – taking notes of key points only, so as not to attract attention.

Do not offer assistance or advice if spoken to, but you can confirm facts. This is the team member's meeting and they must be allowed to make mistakes as this is the basis of the learning experience. Unfortunately, many managers feel compelled to intervene if a client interview is going wrong and they give 'saving the sale' as a reason; this destroys the purpose of the coaching process. At the end of the meeting you should personally thank the client for allowing you to sit in.

Step four – post-activity debriefing

This is where the coaching process takes place, so it is important that the activity is debriefed as soon as possible.

Again, the key is NOT to give your opinion about what was done well or badly – but rather to ask your team member to give their own analysis of:

a) what skills they handled well

and

b) what skills they could have handled more effectively.

Once you have obtained the individual's analysis, you then provide feedback from your observation. This uses the same psychological base as all coaching – if a person defines their own developmental need, they will become more committed to enhancing their performance.

At this point you confirm with the individual what needs to be coached and agree a course of action – either that the coaching will take place immediately, or that a special coaching meeting will be established.

If the individual is an experienced and high-performing member of the team, it is entirely possible that you will not see any skill that could be realistically coached and enhanced. In this case, be careful not to lessen the impact of coaching by trying to find things to coach. Instead, spend the time on motivation or on discussing how the *overall* performance might be enhanced. Experienced people who perform well are always willing to improve their performance but do not respond well to unnecessary coaching.

Managing opportunities for practical application of skills

In seeking to develop a person's performance in a skill and thus their confidence in using it, you will need to manage opportunities for the practical application of the skill or knowledge. It is of little benefit either to the person or the company if no effort is made to place the person in an environment in which they can use their skills – in fact, it would be a complete waste of the investment in that person's development.

Training is expensive and is an investment in people – and all investment must produce a return. In the case of training and coaching, the return must be from enhanced performance and productivity and this leads to enhanced financial return for the company. It is the responsibility of the coach to make sure that this return is delivered and that means managing the opportunities for the new skills to be used. There is little point in spending money on training people if they are then denied the opportunity to make a return on the investment – an investment they have made as well as the one the company has made.

So how do you manage the opportunities for practical application of the skills?

Firstly, you need to make a distinction between newly acquired skills and those that have recently been coached due to incorrect application.

When *newly acquired skills* are first put into operation you should spend all the first day with the newly trained person and should try to ensure that the work they are doing requires the newly acquired skills. As time goes by, you should reduce the period you spend with the person while still trying to manage their work so that they have to use the new skills. This could well result in a slightly false work pattern as specific work is funnelled through to the person so that they can practise the skills. The disruption is worth tolerating as it is the quickest way of bringing a person 'up to speed' with the new skill.

During the time you spend with this person, you will be observing their use of the skill or knowledge and be offering corrective feedback. If that is insufficient, then you will have to offer coaching. Only if that does not work would you consider a short amount of retraining.

When you are dealing with a *recently coached skill* you should still spend regular time with the person to ensure the skill continues to be used correctly. However, there is less reason to try to artificially manage the opportunities for putting the skill into practice. Again, corrective feedback and additional coaching may be required.

Managing the opportunities for skill application is vital but it should never involve setting up an artificial situation – that is valid in a training situation but can often be counter-productive when coaching.

Off-line coaching

In general, coaching takes place 'on-line' – that is, it takes place in the work environment and in real situations. It also takes place with little attempt at privacy, so it is common for others to know when a person is being coached. Since all members of the team should receive regular and frequent coaching, it is seldom a problem to carry out the activity with others around. However, there are occasions and situations when it would be better to offer the coaching in private.

Coaching interpersonal skills

Private, off-line, coaching is particularly beneficial when you are having to coach on *interpersonal skills* and it would be highly embarrassing for someone to receive coaching in front of team mates. Interpersonal skills, as the name suggests, are the skills people use in their everyday dealings with others – they include such things as active listening, handling conflict, dealing with stress, assertive communication, participation in meetings, managing subordinates, managing one's relationship with one's boss.

It has been argued that such things are not in the purview of coaching – some would argue it is not the concern of the company at all – however, interpersonal skills are what allow people to work well together and any failure in this area will have an immediate (and, sometimes, lasting) effect on the performance of the team. This, in its turn, will damage the output of the team and adversely impact on the performance of the company. It is, therefore, a very legitimate area for inclusion in the coaching programme, given that anything that impacts on the company is an area where the company should take action.

The question is: how do you coach interpersonal skills? And the answer has to be: with great care! People are very sensitive to what they perceive as criticism of the way they behave and you will have to position the coaching session carefully. A successful approach is to take the person to one side, preferably into an office or conference room, and be very frank without being critical, aggressive, or insulting. You could say something like this: 'Mary, I notice that you and George don't seem to be communicating in your normal effective manner at the moment. It seems to stem from his reaction to what you've said and I think we should have a look at this to see if you can gain his cooperation more effectively.'

The person *is* going to be defensive – there is no avoiding this – but by using the phrasing above you have indicated:

- that their communication is normally effective

- it is not effective now

- in the circumstances it is a temporary breakdown

- what the cause appears to be

- that this is an opportunity to address the issue.

If you use this approach in an open and friendly manner, you will probably find that the individual is, in some way, relieved to talk about the situation and you can move straight into examining what is the problem and then coaching the skill that is being applied incorrectly. However, there are occasions when you will be met with hostility. You will certainly be told that the problem lies with the other person ('George') and you will have to tread carefully.

The most important thing is to get across the point that you are only concerned about the 'behaviour' exhibited and that you have confidence in the person. If they display aggression or significant resistance to you over this subject you may well have to take a firm line and point out that their behaviour is adversely impacting on their own performance and that of 'George' and possibly the rest of the team. People who are overly sensitive, aggressive or defensive in these circumstances frequently have a genuine problem and it is vital that you probe gently to find out whether:

i) the problem is work-related

or

ii) it is to do with their private life.

If it is work-related – such as lack of confidence or ability, work overload, fear of failing or making an error, dislike of team members, and so on – then you can take steps to rectify the situation before more damage is done. On the other hand, if the problem is in their private life *you have no right to pry and must certainly not become involved.* However, as the problem is affecting the business, you can and should take a sympathetic position, perhaps they could be offered a short time off to resolve the issue or advise them to seek help, and then stress that they must not allow outside problems to adversely impact on their otherwise good performance.

Avoiding disruption

Another occasion when off-line coaching is necessary is
when the actual process of coaching will have a disruptive
effect on the work being done. For example, it is impractical to coach a salesman during a sales call, a bank teller while
they deal with customers, or a manager during a management team meeting. In fact, it is impractical to provide
on-line coaching to anyone whose work involves direct
interaction with customers in particular. Such coaching
should wait until the interaction is complete and the
customer and employee are no longer face to face.

CHAPTER SEVEN

Setting up a coaching programme

The ability of the company to benefit from coaching as a method of developing people is determined to a large extent by the way you set up the coaching programme. It is often extremely difficult to establish the perfect programme as outlined in chapter six and compromises have to be made – especially in terms of who does the coaching – but you should try to get as close to the desirable structure as possible. In this chapter the practical side of establishing a coaching programme is discussed.

The size and scope of the task are what will determine the design of the coaching programme you will need for your company. Once this has been determined, the available resources, in terms of people and budget, will limit the programme and its effect. Keeping these two opposing ideas in mind – the task and the resources – is central to the job of setting up a coaching programme.

Who should be coached?

The first question is: Who needs to be coached? It would be easy just to reply, 'Everyone,' but reality dictates that a more thoughtful analysis is needed.

In coaching terms, the people in touch with the company's customers have to take the highest priority – sales staff, service personnel, customer accounts people and the marketing teams. If these people can have their performance enhanced, then the company will make more money. In many service companies, these people can account for around 30% to 50% of the entire FTE (full-time equivalent) head count. In manufacturing companies the percentage is lower and 10% of the FTE is a possibility.

The second priority is based on a simple assumption: if the customer interface staff are performing better, there should be a greater demand for the products and services of the company and this will require enhanced performance from the manufacturing side and, in a service environment, the operations people. In a service company this could be another 30% to 40% of your FTE and in a manufacturing enterprise the number could be as high as 50% to 70%.

The two top priorities, therefore, amount to between 60% and 90% of a service company and up to 80% of a manufacturing company. The missing percentages cover the head office support and administrative staff and their associated management structures; these form the third priority group.

The next step is to examine each of the priority groups in order and subdivide them. The top priority group, the customer interface staff, can be divided into:

- front-line employees
- their immediate supervisors
- their team leaders or managers
- customer interface support staff
- their supervisors and team leaders
- the functional management teams.

In this selection, the most important people are the front-line employees and their support staff, followed by the two sets of supervisors and team leaders, and finally the functional management teams.

A similar exercise with the manufacturing and operations people will produce similar divisions, as will an examination of the head office and management structure.

123

The cost impact

This prioritisation is necessary if a realistic and cost-effective programme is to be established. If the answer to the question 'Who needs coaching?' is the simplistic 'Everyone,' then a straightforward capacity calculation may well show that it is impracticable. This can be illustrated by the following example:

> If a company employs 100 people then a coaching programme of four days per annum for everyone would require 400 man-days to be devoted to coaching. Given that there are, on average, 220 working days per man-year, you will require 2 people to spend *all* their time on coaching. At an average FTE cost of, say, £20,000 per annum this is around £40,000, which would require an increase in performance worth £400 per person per annum.

The figure of £400 should be very realistic – but it seems doubtful that such a company would be willing to invest £40,000 per annum every year in the development of their people.

On the other hand, it is likely that around 20% of your people are directly involved in producing 80% of the company's revenues. This being the case, if you can identify this 20% you can focus the coaching programme on them – this will require proportionately fewer coaches and thus a proportionally lower investment, while being likely to produce a disproportionately higher return:

> If our company with 100 people has a turnover of £5,000,000 with 20% of the people directly involved in generating 80% of turnover, then 20 people generate £4,000,000 or £200,000 per person. Now, a coaching programme of four days per annum for these

people would cost around £15,000 to £20,000 which would require an increase in performance of just 0.5% per person per annum – which should be very realistic. If they improved their performance by just 10% (a very achievable possibility) then they would each generate an additional £20,000 per person, giving a total increase of £400,000.

Focus on value-generating roles

The financials, therefore, support all the cases for coaching. But in many companies, no matter what their size, senior management will be much happier to accept a programme based on coaching the key 20% of employees.

As demonstrated above, these 20% are likely to be the front-line customer interface people plus their support staff, along with a similar selection among the manufacturing and operations people.

But does this mean the remaining 80% of the company produce no real value for the company? Of course not. Each and every employee has a role to play in the smooth functioning of the enterprise *but they are unlikely to have a significant revenue or turnover-generating role* – in fact, they may not have a revenue or turnover-generating role at all. For example, senior managers seldom generate income for the company but they are necessary if the company is to function – their role is a *value-added* one and not a *value-generating* one. And it is on the *value-generating* roles that we need to concentrate in the initial stages. Only when these people have enhanced their productivity will senior management view a coaching programme for everyone else as realistic.

This is a logical approach and yet it is one that is almost totally ignored by many companies, who focus their coaching on managers first! Managers are not normally in value-generating roles and, providing they are doing their jobs reasonably well, they should not form part of the initial phase of the coaching programme.

A successful coaching programme will, therefore, focus initially on the percentage of the FTE head count that is in the key value-generating roles, and identifying these people must be your top priority. Once coaching is fully established for these people, the programme can and should be expanded to cover the rest of the customer interface people and the manufacturing or operations people, including their managers. Head office-type functions and other management will have to wait until the third phase.

What has to be coached?

The second step in determining the task is to consider exactly what has to be coached. Once again, there is the simplistic answer 'everything', and once again this answer needs to be examined critically.

Taking your key selection of *value-generating* people, you will need to look carefully at what they should be doing – this may be different from what they are doing – and this will reveal what activities and skills are most likely to enhance their ability to deliver *value generation*. These activities and skills are what really need to be coached, along with any basic skills that are being applied incorrectly.

Once you have completed this analysis, you will have identified: (a) the key people to be coached, and (b) the activities and skills that need to be enhanced.

You now have the scope of the task you face.

However, no allowance has been made for the fact that many of the people you will have identified are already delivering a satisfactory or above satisfactory performance. This is an 'opportunity' within the programme which eases the pressure on the coaches.

How much coaching?

The third step is to identify the optimum coaching levels you wish to see in the company. Are you going to go for a programme of one day per month per person? One day per quarter per person? Two half days per quarter? An 'as-needed' approach? Or one involving continuous monitoring and action? Each of these has an impact on your capacity to deliver the programme as they will determine the number of people needed as coaches. *A good guide is that everyone chosen for coaching should have a total of one day's coaching per quarter with additional coaching as needed.*

With these steps complete, you are now in a position to determine the time required in man-days to carry out the proposed coaching. This will, of course, determine how many coaches you will actually need – and this should be costed just in case you decide to employ people in this role rather than finding them from within the organisation.

What skills and attributes should a coach have?

The question of who should be the coach is extremely fundamental. Appointing the wrong person can eliminate the benefits of the coaching almost entirely and it is worth making a very careful choice based on what the coach has to do and what skills and attributes the person will need to do the job successfully. Making this choice is no different, in terms of what needs to be done, from selecting anyone to carry out any role within the organisation.

Skills

The skills needed to be a successful coach can be broken down into three groups.

Communication

The main skill needed is that of being a good communicator. The ability to listen actively and provide accurate feedback on what you have understood, to be able to communicate ideas clearly, understandably, and in a friendly manner, and to be able to use words in such a way that you lead people to discover for themselves what they need to know, and need to do, is absolutely vital. It is very little use just telling people what to do as this seldom leads to a genuine understanding.

This ability goes further than speaking and listening skills – it must also encompass the non-verbal communication that exists between people. Behavioural scientists have concluded that up to 80% of communication is non-verbal – 'body language' as the popular phrase puts it. Coaches must demonstrate good non-verbal communication if their coaching is to be effective.

Also under the heading of communication is the ability to present complex matters in a way that others can grasp. In this case, it is better to show and lead rather than tell – it is only when a person being coached can connect each element of the process that they will be able to deliver that process correctly. Coaches, therefore, must be able to use a probing and questioning style so that they are able to draw from the other person the connections in, and thus their understanding of, the process.

Acting

Good acting skills are also a major advantage. One of the quickest ways of coaching a skill is to role-play the process and this requires acting skills. The better the coach is at this, the easier it is for the other person to get into the spirit of the session and to practise the skill.

This does not mean that every coach should be seeking an Oscar for their performance, but they should be good enough to take the role of all the people involved in the process being coached. Role-plays are used a lot in the course of training workshops but they can also be used in coaching *even when the skill to be coached is a physical skill such as operating a piece of equipment*. Knowing when to demonstrate the skill and its correct and incorrect usage is a vital part of coaching.

Practical knowledge

It is impossible to deliver coaching without knowledge of the process. You do not have to be an expert in the skill but you must have a thorough understanding – intellectually – of how the skill works.

Attributes

Certain personal attributes are also necessary if a coach is to be successful.

Task focus

The singularly most important attribute is that of task focus. Coaches who have no task focus fail to deliver their responsibilities. This is an obvious point to make, but consider: the coach has the responsibility to ensure that all elements of a process or skill are delivered correctly and yet the *task* is often to correct a small part of the application of the skill. The coach has therefore to be particularly focused on the part that needs correction and must not be side-tracked into just looking at the process as a whole. All too often people try to coach the whole process rather than focusing on the real task.

Patience

It can be terribly frustrating for a coach when a person cannot grasp a skill, but it is vital that frustration does not appear. The coach must be very patient with a person who is relearning a skill – getting rid of bad habits is not easy. What is simple to someone who is already skilled in something is not simple at all to those who are not yet skilled, or are misusing a skill. (That is why they need coaching.)

Humour

Humour, appropriately used, is a great tension-reliever. Although some of the best coaches have been humourless men and women, those who have a ready sense of the absurd and can see the funny side of even the most difficult situations have a major advantage when helping people develop their skills. The danger is in using humour inappropriately and making the other person feel that you are laughing at them – that just builds resentment which is counter-productive. But using humour appropriately and deliberately to ease tensions will make the learning and coaching process easier.

Professionalism and professional pride

If you demonstrate professionalism and take pride in it then this will communicate itself to the other person, no matter how uncomfortable they are with the coaching situation. Your professionalism indicates that the situation is purely one of professional development, it is nothing personal, and that the other person should also take pride in their professional actions. After all, you are both professionals. This focus on professionalism – on the job in hand and the company you are working for – will make it possible for people to accept coaching for what it is: a process for assisting others to develop their skills and enhance their own professional performance.

Identifying the coaches

For the vast majority of companies, the only accessible source of coaches is within the organisation – mainly managers, direct supervisors and the training department – but these people cannot be taken away from their day-to-day work for extended periods of time without it affecting their own performance. On the other hand, if the coaching programme is to be successful, enough hours have to be set aside to cover the key people you have selected as being most able to benefit the company by having their performance enhanced.

The dilemma is not easy to resolve. The simplistic answer is that each manager and direct supervisor will have to be involved and will have to coach their team; but this ignores the fact that many managers and supervisors are fully loaded as far as work is concerned; and they may not be suitable people to have as coaches. A better approach might be to identify those supervisors and managers who could coach certain *ranges of skills* – these people, providing they have the right skills and attributes to be coaches, could then be trained.

If the latter approach is used, and this may be in the best interests of the company, then you will also have to identify whether these people have spare capacity or whether they need to be freed up by their superiors so that they can take on different responsibilities while, at the same time, maintaining many of their original ones. The important thing here is to stress that the coaching they will be undertaking will not be an *additional* responsibility – that would be unreasonable – but, rather, it is a *different* responsibility. This, of course, may well mean that some of their original functions and responsibilities will have to be passed to others. This change in responsibilities could be considered as a 'promotion' of sorts and a step towards fuller management responsibility.

You must also establish a method of ensuring that the new responsibility for coaching is delivered. This suggests that it will be necessary to include coaching as part of a redefined job description (one that also shows that other responsibilities have been reassigned) and to attach Minimum Performance Standards (MPS) to the activity. It will also be necessary to ensure that senior management is fully aware of the new responsibilities and that they appraise performance accordingly.

But where will you find the person who will be a successful coach? The answer has to be: 'just about anywhere'. But not necessarily where you might expect.

Direct supervisors

Probably the most common source of coaches, the direct supervisors, are appointed because they are thought to be the best suited to overseeing the development of the people below them. But is this true?

The advantage of using supervisors is that they are in direct contact with their people on a day-to-day basis and should be able to spot a decline in performance or an inappropriately applied skill straight away. They are also generally the most skilled in the processes involved – which is often why they are the supervisor – but does this make them the best people to act as coaches?

Supervisors are often in that role as a result of seniority rather than managerial or leadership ability. Their role is to see that the job gets done and they, themselves, are frequently an essential part of the process. They are tasked with the smooth running of a small part of the team and meeting the sub-team's goals. They *are* in a position to observe their team (they have a direct responsibility to do so) and they should be watching for situations in which coaching would benefit the performance of the group; but their main responsibility has to be making sure the process is working. If they see coaching is needed then they should report the matter and get a coach in.

Although most people like to help others, and supervisors are no exception in this, they frequently do not have the right skills and attributes to be good coaches. Left to their own devices, supervisors will ensure that their team is performing well and that each person is carrying out their function as efficiently as possible, but it is a rare supervisor who will have the time or inclination to get involved in skill-development. And it is unlikely to be to the supervisor's or the company's advantage if the supervisor fails to deliver their quota of the work.

There will be some supervisors who would make excellent coaches – in which case a decision has to be made as to whether they should be relieved of some of their work in order to have the time to coach. If the answer is that the goals require the supervisors' full output then it would be unrealistic to expect them to spend time coaching. If supervisors are to coach then they must have their own goals adjusted to reflect this.

Finally, supervisors are often people who have been with the team for a long time and have worked their way up, and while the team accepts the person in a supervisory role, they may be less willing to accept coaching from them.

Managers and team leaders

In many companies these are the people who have the direct responsibility to act as coaches for their team. But is this the right approach?

A manager or team leader has direct responsibility for the delivery of their team's goals and to do this they must make very sure that each peson in the team is delivering a performance that will allow this to happen. Clearly, therefore, the manager or team leader should be watching for declines in performance or inappropriately applied skills and to address the issue straight away.

The manager's main job responsibility is the team and its goals but does that mean they have either the time or the skills to act as a coach? More and more, the role of manager is becoming the role of supervisor – that is, one of the team, with personal-output goals to be achieved. One of the reasons why many companies have successfully 'delayered' their management structure is that managers as team *leaders* are no longer the real requirement and the term 'manager' has become a misnomer. The manager as a team *member* with additional responsibilities is closer to the reality; in which case their suitability will be the same as that of supervisor, discussed above.

In such circumstances, senior management – those with direct responsibility for the delivery of company goals – must take responsibility for the leadership function and, with it, the responsibility for the development of performance through coaching. But the question remains: are *they* the best qualified, and do they have the time?

Members of the training department

The first thing to acknowledge here is that not every company has a training department. For those companies that do, the question is: should trainers also act as coaches?

Most training department people would say that they are so understaffed and overcommitted that there is no way that they could take on the role of coach: however, this avoids the question. If pushed, the same people would probably say that trainers would make good coaches and there is clear justification for this. If you compared your list of skills and attributes for a coach with that of a trainer, you would find many matching characteristics and a significant correlation beween the two functions.

There are arguments against trainers fulfilling the role of coaches – conflict of objectives, blurring of distinction between the two functions and so on – but there are far more arguments *for* the arrangement. However, to make it a reality requires a rethink about the human resources strategy of the company. Most companies see the training depart-ment as a purely tactical operation whereas, in reality, it is a strategic tool. The principal objective of the training team is to deliver the training necessary for the company to reach its strategic goal. And it goes further: training is a long-term strategic tool − training is too expensive to be used for purely tactical reasons and it takes too long to train up a person to fulfil a skilled role for short-termism to have any part to play.

If this dichotomy in management thinking can be elimi-nated then the strategic role of training will allow the training department to formulate long-term plans that recognise the importance of coaching. This, in turn, would lead to the establishment of coaching programmes that would be resourced by the training department and oper-ated by the team leaders.

Would this be a good thing? Yes, it would − it's not an ideal solution but it is certainly a practical and effective one. The team leaders would still have to take responsibility for positive and corrective feedback as they are the ones who should see and could act on the opportunities for this, but the coaching of particular skills could be formulated into the programme with trainer-coaches circulating through the company all the time.

There is also a major additional benefit: trainers as coaches would mean that the trainers would be spending a good percentage of their time in the front line with real situations and this would enhance their knowledge and thus enhance the training they would be delivering. This, in turn, provides another benefit: the coaches would be able to track the problems that occur regularly or frequently in the appli-cation of skills and knowledge, and could move to enhance the relevant training course to provide additional focus on these areas and so diminish the 'down time' in the future.

Specialist internal coaches

This is, probably, the best solution for those companies that don't have training departments or have ones that are understaffed. In every organisation there are people who have specialist knowledge of certain processes and skills and these people could be trained to act as coaches to be called in whenever there is a need. Normally, such people would be quite senior, either in terms of length of service or function, and would have the credibility to deliver specialist coaching. For example, a senior salesperson could be used as a coach on sales processes, the marketing manager could coach front-line managers in micro-marketing activity, senior credit officers could add value by coaching credit staff in distant offices, materials engineers could coach on the properties of materials being machined, senior financial controllers could add value by coaching front-line and departmental managers on their budget preparations and reporting – the list is almost endless. Remember that in each case, the specialist coach would have to be given the *time* to fulfil their coaching responsibilities.

Sending such senior people out as coaches will provide them with the opportunity to acquire feedback on the working of the organisation and how things in their areas could be improved. These visits will also provide a boost to the motivation of the people being coached.

There has been considerable talk during the mid 1990s on the concept of the 'learning organisation' – an organisation that continuously obtains new knowledge about itself and its markets – and what better way for this to happen than to have senior management circulating throughout the business in a coaching and listening role?

Specialist external coaches

This is a much more difficult subject but it is another solution for those companies that do not have training departments at all. Unfortunately, specialists from outside are, by the very nature of being outside the company, unable to coach on internal and non-generic activities. Of course, a specialist lathe operator could be called in to coach the lathe operators, because lathe operating is a generic process – every company that has lathes needs them to be operated in broadly the same way. And the same applies to fork-lift truck drivers, digger drivers and crane operators. Indeed, when dealing with a generic skill – one that everyone doing that job has to have no matter who they work for – it may be cheaper to have an external coach than to set up an internal coaching programme.

But some generic processes – sales, for example – lend themselves to the use of external coaches only up to a point. When company-specific products are involved and the need for product-specific knowledge is a must, then the external coach is limited in their ability to add value. This should not act as a barrier to the use of external coaches but should be recognised as requiring a solution.

External coaches are also a good source of support for management development – a situation where the more senior the person, the more likely they are to resent coaching and, therefore, the more likely they are to accept it from an outside expert who presents no 'political' threat to them. It has to be recognised that senior managers are unlikely to find anyone *within* the company who is in a position to coach them - those who could coach are too senior to be involved with development activity (or think they are!) or they are too junior for either party to feel comfortable with a coaching situation.

Line managers – An imperfect solution in a business environment

Many companies are not equipped to have specially selected coaches and many more do not have the budget; and yet research shows that almost all companies see coaching as a vital part of their development and the development of their people. So how is this dilemma to be resolved? How can and how do these companies establish coaching without using specially trained coaches? The answer is simply that they have decided that line managers should carry out the role as part of their overall responsibilities. This is not likely to be a perfect solution but it may be the only one available and, with the proper support, it can be, and often is, surprisingly effective. The key to using line managers as coaches is recognition of the fact that development of the individuals in the team is a *prime responsibility* of their manager or leader.

All managers have three primary responsibilities: (a) achieving the task they and their team have been set, (b) assembling and developing the team to carry out the task, and (c) developing the individuals so that they deliver the necessary performance for the team to achieve its task. Coaching is the main way that a manager can ensure that individuals deliver the necessary performance and thus coaching can be considered a primary responsibility of all managers. The problem is that very few managers see coaching as *their* responsibility and even fewer senior managers consider putting coaching into their subordinates' job description. Without some focus on coaching as a job requirement, coaching will just not get done.

The failure to enshrine coaching in their job descriptions means that, day to day, managers make their own decisions as to what is important and inevitably they focus on the short term – such as delivering the numbers – and ignore the long-term requirements that will ensure the success of the company in an ever-changing world. On the other hand, if senior managers took a strategic and long-term view they would recognise the importance of their people delivering both for today and for the future. They would ensure that development of key people takes a high priority, equally weighted with delivering the task in terms of overall performance.

The prerequisites to enable line managers to act as coaches are therefore:

■ to include coaching in the line manager's job description as a primary responsibility

■ to establish a coaching programme throughout the company so that everyone is aware of the requirement and what is expected

■ to train the managers as coaches

■ to establish that senior management will oversee the coaching programme.

The coaching guide

Having identified the coaches, you should now write down exactly how the programme is supposed to operate. This process will allow you to identify any areas you have not yet addressed as well as producing a 'guide book' for the coaches themselves. The one thing you do *not* want to do is to write an operating manual – coaching is a dynamic process that requires considerable flexibility and you should keep the guide as a simple outline of actions that have to be under-taken and who is involved. Remember, you still have to inform the key employees and if the guide becomes a manual you will find it much harder to obtain their commitment to the programme.

One possible approach would be to restrict the guide to a three-page memo to everyone involved, including the senior management. The memo would cover:

■ what is to be done

■ who is to do the coaching

■ how frequently it is to take place

- the purpose of the coaching
- the expected results
- how the programme is to be monitored and measured.

The memo is initially circulated to those chosen as coaches as this encourages them to feel that they have become part of a special-project group and, in turn, this causes them to develop a certain group-togetherness leading to higher levels of motivation. You can then obtain their commitment which makes it easier to 'sell' the programme to those who are to be coached.

As it is vital to engage all participants in the process, you cannot just announce the programme and expect it to be successful. One successful approach is to send every-one involved the outline of the plan and, *at the same time*, invite them to a meeting so that you can outline the programme in greater detail, introduce all the coaches, and address the concerns of the participants. And they will have concerns! Questions may even be hostile. But patience and clear communication of the benefits to those involved, as well as the benefits to the company, will generally carry the day. Please note: you have to stress the benefits to those involved – on the whole the people to be coached are not particularly interested in the benefits to the company but they are interested in the benefits to themselves.

One question that always arises is: will the enhanced performance attract rewards, or, put another way, will they get paid more for producing more? This could be difficult to explain – especially if the company has a policy of not giving salary enhancements. You can address this concern ('what's in it for me?') by stressing the greater job satisfaction that enhanced performance gives, the improved prospects for advancement within the company, and the recognition that these people are the key employees of the firm – the top 20%. This will not satisfy everyone, especially if you have a unionised environment, but most people want to feel better about themselves and this programme is one way of delivering this.

One benefit to the company that is sometimes a desirable benefit to the individuals is that, once their own performance is fully enhanced, they too could be eligible to join the programme as a coach. This can be seen as an upgrading of their role in the company and, combined with the natural tendency of individuals to help each other, can lead to even greater commitment to the programme. Of course, care has to be taken in asking these key employees to assist as coaches – they are not likely to be allowed to travel or to work with other groups or teams but they could be very useful within their own team. Care must also be taken to ensure that those key employees who might become coaches actually have the right attributes – the skills can be taught where necessary.

Measuring the effectiveness of the programme

Just as training is an investment in people, so is coaching, and, like all investments, a coaching programme must show a return. This is especially true if the programme is to be funded and supported by senior management. It is vital, therefore, that the effectiveness of the programme can be measured.

Since the objective of the programme is to enhance performance, the first step is to identify the current performance of the people who are to be coached. With sales people this is relatively simple – you could measure how many sales they make in a given period or how many new customers they bring in. But even with sales people it can be extremely difficult to establish performance criteria in some companies. This is often the result of too great a focus on financials (MIS) and the short-term bottom line and not enough focus on the criteria that tell you how your people are doing.

You should start with the Minimum Performance Standards associated with the job and then look at the Performance Enhancing Goals that have been established; these will certainly give you an idea of what is likely to be affected by the coaching programme and thus what must be measured. This is not the same as saying that there are methods of measuring these things currently in place. And when you step away from the direct customer-interface people it is very probable that no method of measuring performance has ever been established. At this point you may be tempted to ignore the situation and just launch the coaching programme – however, this would be a major wrong step.

Knowing where you are at the moment is vital if you are to measure the difference between current and future performance and it is this difference that is the measure of the effectiveness of the programme. The absolute numbers are not relevant here, only the incremental change. You are, after all, looking to improve performance – by 10% or by 25% or by $20,000 per annum per person. This highlights a second point: you need to be able to measure the change in performance at various levels: the *individual*, the *company*, and the *team*.

Measuring the change in performance

These are the three absolutes that have to be measured: the change in performance of each *individual*, the change in performance of the *team* or *unit*, and the change in performance of the *company*. What other changes are measured must be a business decision governed by the company itself.

But you would be advised to measure only the key things in each case *unless there is very sophisticated MIS data available.* You are, after all, trying to improve performance through coaching and not trying to redesign the entire company MIS system.

The common factor in all the chosen measurements is that they must be easy to do and represent a monitoring of actual performance of the individuals and the teams. This will almost automatically lead to improved financial returns. By using these performance measures throughout the coaching programme you are able to monitor the *change* in performance that defines the effectiveness of the programme itself.

But what about manufacturing departments? Again, you must ensure that what is measured is the performance that will be affected by the coaching programme and not some abstract indicator that is of interest to management but has little to do with the performance of the individuals and the team. This is especially important when considering financial indicators − these are of little benefit since they are totally outside the control of the individuals and teams. It is imperative that new programmes should not add to the burden of monitoring and reporting.

Managerial resistance to monitoring

When performance monitoring is first introduced it is often met with considerable resistance by just about everyone. This resistance declines very rapidly among team members once they understand *what* is being monitored, *why* it is being monitored, *how* it is being monitored and *where* it is being monitored. This last point is very important − people need to trust the source of the data, especially if it is being used to enhance performance through goals or is used as part of an evaluation or appraisal system.

What is interesting is that the greatest resistance to monitoring is often found amongst the front-line and middle management. The reasons given are generally:

■ monitoring is too time-consuming

■ it doesn't relate to the goals that I have to deliver

■ in my team, performance is too difficult to measure

■ my team wouldn't like it

■ my people are professionals and don't need this sort of thing.

What they are really saying is, 'I don't know how to manage for performance; I'm not a leader, I am part of the team and its process, and I don't understand the positive impact of monitoring.' They are also declaring that it is easier to do things the old way rather than the right way (that might bring them to the attention of *their* boss). Unfortunately, this is a common problem that can only be rectified through the provision of professional training for all new managers and the coaching of those currently in position.

Whatever the reaction of the managers and supervisors, it is vital that performance monitoring is established as this is the *only* way that the effectiveness of the coaching programme can be measured.

'Monitoring is too time-consuming'

Monitoring certainly takes a certain amount of time. The time allocation is, however, heaviest in setting up the monitoring and making sure everyone knows what it is, what it is for and how it is to be operated and displayed. Once this is done the actual process of monitoring takes only minutes per day at the most and, since everyone gets a motivational boost from seeing how they are doing, it is generally best left to the individuals to operate. The objection that people will cheat is more an expression of a lack of trust by the manager than a real situation and accuracy and honesty have to be assumed – if they are, they will become a reality, which is another reason why monitoring must be introduced well before the coaching programme starts.

Managers and supervisors who use the time requirement as an excuse are often expressing their own fear that by carrying out monitoring their own performance as a leader will be shown up. This is understandable and identifies an area that must be addressed when coaching the managers.

To overcome the 'time' objection you will probably have to help the person identify the performance criteria to be monitored and help them set up the process. You will also need to make sure that it is being carried out properly.

'It doesn't relate to the goals that I have to deliver'
This is a very common objection and suggests that the manager or supervisor has not thought through the various components that make up the goals that they have to deliver. This very understandable situation arises mainly because managers and supervisors are not encouraged to study the processes of their teams in an analytical manner, which would allow them to identify the key performance areas.

If you are faced with this situation you should help the manager understand how the process works so that they can identify the elements that go to make up the goals they have to deliver. You must then show them how an incremental improvement in the performance in each area will lead to an overall improvement in the team's performance.

145

'In my team, performance is too difficult to measure'
This again demonstrates a lack of understanding of the elements that make up the overall team performance. As with the previous objection, you tackle it by helping them identify all the elements.

'My team wouldn't like it'
This objection is based on the personal insecurity of the manager or supervisor on the basis of their authority and their role of leader or manager.

It is very possible that the team members may not like the idea of performance monitoring, but once they understand it and why it is being done they should soon accept it and even be active and enthusiastic participants.

The manager must also be brought to understand that it is their direct responsibility – as the team leader or manager – to ensure that their team is working to maximum performance and this can only be done if the team's performance is monitored. It is, therefore, their direct responsibility to monitor performance, and their authority to put monitoring in place is derived from their position.

'My people are professionals and don't need this sort of thing'
This is a direct refusal by the manager to accept the responsibility of their position and to understand their role. Putting it bluntly, if the team does not need performance management and all that that entails – such as performance monitoring, coaching, and so on – then they do not need a supervisor or manager. In which case, the manager can be reassigned out of the team, or even out of the company.

Obviously, you are not likely to put it quite like that and you will coach them and help them understand their role and to accept its responsibilities, but you should keep in mind that any manager raising this objection is possibly out of their depth or not committed to delivering performance

– they may even be experts at 'make-work' and are, in fact, not productive at all.

Whatever the reason given, managerial resistance to monitoring is generally a sign that the manager needs training or coaching.

PART THREE: MENTORING

For long-term development and performance

The long-term survival and success of a company depends, to a considerable extent, on the long-term commitment of the staff. And that commitment is dependent on how well you develop them. Quite a few companies feel that, once they have delivered the main training programmes and provided the necessary coaching, there is nothing more they have to do. They are wrong – especially when dealing with those workers carrying out intellectual rather than physical work. Such people need and expect constant and continuous development – something that is best handled through mentoring.

Mentoring is a stand-alone programme for those members of staff whose long-term development is very much in the best interests of the company. The programme contains elements of both training and coaching but it is much more than an extension of skills development. In mentoring we are looking at the development of the whole person in their own and the company's best interests.

In the following two chapters we will be looking at:

■ What mentoring is

■ Setting up a mentoring programme

CHAPTER EIGHT

What is mentoring?

The problems to be solved

Mentoring is a solution to the problem that faces most companies today – that employees are no longer willing to stay with a company for long periods of their working career. Indeed, such adherence to one employer is no longer viewed favourably as companies seek to engage new talent and bring in new ideas to help boost performance. This applies to all staff – managers and other staff alike.

Employment surveys carried out by recruitment consultants have found that managers stay with their first company for just five years. Subsequent moves tend to occur at regular intervals of about seven years and once the person reaches senior management they either work out their days with the final company or are head-hunted at three-yearly intervals. A similar pattern is now becoming apparent with skilled technical workers, supervisory and junior management, and front-line customer interface staff.

Why is this a problem? Beside the obvious disruption caused by frequent changes of personnel, the other major impact is economic, and both lead to a decline in company performance. Consider, for example, managers: they are paid high salaries and, quite reasonably, their company expects a return on the investment. But new managers are unlikely to be effective in the role until they have obtained sufficient knowledge about the company and the job to be able to make a realistic contribution. This can take anything from a couple of months to nearly a year and during this time the manager is costing the company in performance terms. If they are then going to move on after five years, they are likely to spend much of their fifth year with the company seeking a new job and thus again not be focused on their current activity and performance. The obvious conclusion is that, in a five-year period, the manager gains five years of experience whereas the company gains only a little over three years of *value-added* activity.

The problem is made worse if the company has provided serious management training – in this case they are, effectively, training managers for their competitors. This has a serious financial impact within the company – a week's management training *every year for five years* has a fully loaded cost of around £50,000 but the company sees little in the way of a return. To put this in perspective, in a five-year period the company is likely to have invested six years' salary to obtain just three years' work. This also applies to non-management staff.

To combat this, companies are now seeking ways to link pay with performance. Career paths are more clearly defined with specified training and development programmes – if a person wants a promotion or additional responsibility, then they must undertake the necessary training and deliver the performance that will encourage senior management to entrust them with greater responsibility and higher pay.

While such an approach will benefit both the individual and the company, it does become rather complex in terms of human resource management and it risks becoming very bureaucratic. To address this, companies are turning to the process called mentoring.

Mentoring can be used with any member of staff but it is most common within what is loosely referred to as 'the management structure'. It is a system in which a more senior manager takes direct responsibility for overseeing the development of another, more junior manager. An effective mentoring system within a company has both practical and financial advantages but it does need to be properly structured with adequate checks and controls to ensure that it results in enhancement of performance. This is the subject of chapter nine. However, to set up an *effective* mentoring programme you must first of all have a clear understanding of:

■   the basic principle of mentoring

■   the responsibilities of the mentor to the company and to the individual

■   the responsibilities of the person being mentored toward the mentor and themself.

The basic principle of mentoring

The basic principle is simple enough: in order to avoid the inherent problems associated with the normal senior manager/junior manager relationship as far as personal development is concerned, a senior manager *in a different reporting line* is given responsibility for mentoring one or more junior colleagues with whom they would not normally have contact.

Senior managers, such as department heads or function heads, generally have a number of other managers reporting to them. In many companies the average is probably between three and five. These junior managers are in charge of operating teams within the department and may have a significantly higher number of people reporting to them either directly or through supervisors. The more hierarchical the company, the more layers of management are involved but most have only three layers between function head and front-line workers as illustrated in Figure 8.1.

The problem, in developmental terms, is that the function head should be responsible for developing their three directly reporting managers as people-managers, but it is likely that the head has too many responsibilities to be able

153

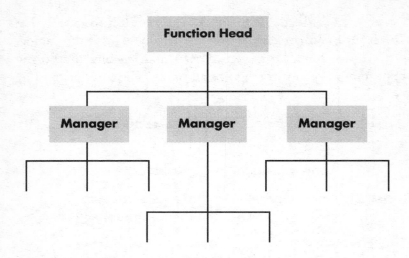

Fig. 8.1 A typical management structure

to spend adequate time on this important aspect of their work. In addition, the three reporting managers are directly responsible for controlling the work of the department and thus delivering the departmental goals. It is possible, therefore, that they will be under a certain amount of pressure from the function head and this may preclude a mentoring relationship. This is where a company mentoring programme comes in: the responsibility for the development of the three managers would be switched from the function head to a manager in a different reporting line. This is illustrated in Figure 8.2.

To be truly effective there would a different mentor for each of the three managers so as to avoid any possible conflict of authority between the mentor and the function head. The mentors work closely with the function head as well as the people they are mentoring to ensure that the objectives of the mentoring programme are achieved without interfering with the delivery of the department's goals. This allows the function head to have an input into the development process without the inherent issues of the

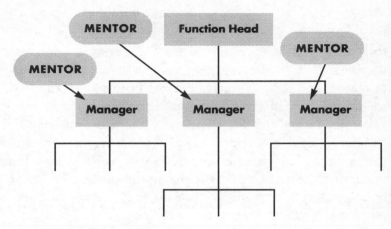

Fig. 8.2 A typical mentoring structure

relationship getting in the way; at the same time, the work of the department is not disrupted.

Who is mentored?

It is possible to arrange mentoring for all managers up to, but not including, the senior management team.

The mentor must always be more senior to those being mentored and, preferably, older as this makes it easier for those receiving advice to accept it. It is human nature to resent advice being given by someone perceived as being younger or less experienced although youthful 'experts' are accepted when the subject is technical.

All companies have, as their primary objective, the goal of making profits – of making returns on the capital invested. This means that hard decisions have to be made concerning the investment made in developing any member of staff – will the time, effort and money involved generate an adequate return within a reasonable period? This is the reality of the business world: if your mentoring programme is to be successful, certain practical considerations and constraints need to be taken into account.

155

Working within such constraints means that you will have to decide at an early stage which of the managers are to be involved in the programme. For example, you could decide that only those managers who have demonstrated potential for senior management positions should be included – a 'fast-track' approach. You may take a more general view and include all managers. Equally, you may feel the need to make a selection based on different criteria. If the potential budget is limited, then you will have to adopt selection criteria that puts the maximum number of people in the programme with the proviso that they are the ones who can make the biggest impact for the company.

The mentor's responsibilities

A mentor's responsibilities fall into two categories: (a) responsibility to the company and (b) responsibility to the person being mentored.

Responsibility to the company

The purpose of the mentoring programme is to bring out the best in the individuals *so that they can contribute more effectively to the performance of the company*. There are those who would argue that a development programme is for the benefit of the individual but this is only partially true. In corporate terms, a development programme must, primarily, benefit the company. The company is there to make money and all activities it enters into must benefit the company as much as, if not more than, the individuals. This is a reality of business. The mentoring activity, therefore, has to have measurable performance goals associated with the objectives of the programme and the company.

The primary objective must be to enhance the individual's ability to deliver a *value-added* performance – in this way, the company can expect to receive the benefit of improved productivity. This improved productivity is best obtained through development of (i) individual skills associated with carrying out the role more effectively, and (ii) people-management skills.

Effective work skills

The important thing to remember is that it is *not* the responsibility of the mentor to *deliver* the training or the coaching but to define what development work needs to be done. The mentor should also assist the individual in obtaining the training or coaching needed and, most importantly, to agree the performance criteria and how it will be measured. For example, the performance criteria should include a time limit for completion of the development work, and should define the necessary standard. At the end of the allotted period of time, the mentor should carry out a further observation to ensure that the improvements have been achieved. It is also the responsibility of the mentor, in conjunction with the manager's superior, to determine what technical training and coaching is still required so that the person is delivering their responsibilities at the correct level. Again, it is not the mentor's responsibility to deliver the training but to ensure that it is undertaken.

People-management skills

When it comes to people-management skills, the mentor may be tempted to actually deliver the training and coaching but this should be resisted – the mentor is there to oversee the development and will have their own workload to consider. Thus the mentor acts very much as a 'godfather' or 'godmother'.

In determining development needs in the area of people-management, the mentor needs to obtain input not only from the individual concerned and their superior, but also from the people directly reporting to them – their team – and from the mentored person's colleagues and anyone else

157

in the organisation that the person comes in contact with on a regular basis.

This acquisition of information is often seen by the person as threatening and it is vital for the relationship between the mentor and the individual that it should be fully understood by everyone concerned. It is not uncommon to come across situations in which there was a clear lack of understanding concerning the mentoring programme. This leads to questions such as: Why was the mentor asking questions? What concern is a manager's work to a senior manager from a different department? If the mentoring programme is properly communicated to everyone in the company then resistance is less and people are far more willing to help in the development of others.

Responsibility to the individual

Perhaps the greatest responsibility a mentor has to their 'godson' or 'goddaughter' is to ensure that they understand that the role of the mentor involves responsibilities both to the company and to the individual, and that the purpose of a mentoring programme is to enhance the value of the individual to the company.

Initial learning curve

One of the most powerful contributions that a mentor can make is to facilitate the initial learning curve that a manager has to go through when they first take on a new role. It can take anything from a couple of months to a year before the manager is fully familiar with their new role and is making a full contribution to the company. The mentor can speed up this process.

Part of the familiarisation process is learning who does what and who to talk to in order to get things done. This is especially true if the manager is new to the company or division. The mentor can make things easier by guiding the individual in this quest for knowledge. Speeding the assimilation of the manager into the organisation will bring benefits to the company but will also enable the individual to settle down more quickly and to gain confidence.

Confessor and confidant(e)

Like everyone else, managers need someone they can talk to about their professional day-to-day problems. There are few corporate cultures that encourage managers to share their problems with their superiors – managers are thought to be beyond that sort of thing – but it is often the need to share problems and the lack of opportunity to do this that leads to a failure to perform adequately. The mentor can play a major role here as 'confessor' or confidant(e) – the person to whom the junior manager can turn without feeling they are demonstrating weakness, lack of confidence or lack of ability.

Everyone needs a confidant(e) with whom to talk through their problems and to whom they can express their frustrations and concerns. And this person must respect those confidences and keep them confidential. Some people are lucky and their immediate superior is able to play this role, but it is far more likely that neither party will be comfortable with this. The mentor is there for just such a purpose. Indeed, there are many people who think that is all the mentor has to do. And, even if they do nothing else, the mentor will deliver a valuable service by listening and advising where necessary.

Playing the role of confessor or confidant(e) requires patience and an ability to listen actively without giving into the very human temptation to offer advice all the time. Often, people need only to talk about their problems in order to find a solution, and it is the solutions people find for themselves that are the most valuable. So the mentor must draw from the manager all the details of the problem and encourage them to face the facts and to find an answer.

This is not as easy as it sounds, given that a more experienced person may well feel they know the best way of handling a situation but must still allow the junior manager to find that solution for themselves. The mentor may not always be right – different strategies may work for different people.

For the mentor to play this role successfully, they will need to build trust with those they are mentoring – people will only share their concerns with their mentor if they believe the mentor will keep them confidential. This means that the mentor must also refrain from taking actions on their behalf unless specifically requested to. Again, this is not easy as the mentor may feel that taking some sort of action is in the best interests of the company – however, if this is the case, they must first obtain the agreement of the 'godchild' if the mentoring relationship is to be protected.

The confessor role can also present other challenges such as what to do when it becomes clear that the junior manager is having problems in their relationship with their superior. This is not as straightforward to deal with as some may imagine. The mentor can hardly go to the junior manager's boss and say that there is an interpersonal clash. Obviously, the mentor will attempt to advise the individual on how to 'manage upwards', how to handle their relationship with their boss. However, if the problem is affecting the performance of the manager and team, then careful steps will have to be taken to try and rectify the situation.

Confidentiality

Both the individual and those providing information about the individual's performance must trust the mentor to keep it confidential. The information is only for the mentor and must be used only to design a development programme and must never be used as part of any performance appraisal. In addition, the source of the information must also remain confidential so as not to cause interpersonal problems.

Confidentiality in the mentoring relationship is vital and must be considered a major responsibility.

Personal coach

Although the mentor is not supposed to deliver the training and coaching needed, there are times when the mentor's responsibility to the individual requires that they act as coach. Most often this occurs when the person wants to prepare for an important meeting – especially with senior management – and needs to discuss the content and style of presentation that will be used. The mentor is likely to have a good idea of how their colleagues will respond to the information and style of presentation and can coach the individual accordingly while, at the same time, stressing that they are neither supporting nor disagreeing with the position being taken.

Some mentors find this difficult to pull off and tend towards either playing it safe or trying to refocus the content to what they believe. Either approach is unfair to the individual – they must be exposed to the competitiveness of management debate as part of their development and the mentor's job is simply to help them to make the presentation as professional as possible.

Another occasion when personal coaching may be called for is when the individual needs assistance in managing others, especially their boss. The mentor's greater experience and different point of view will enable them to offer coaching on how to say or write things in such a way that a more positive result can be expected.

Career director

Another valuable role the mentor can play is as the director or overseer of a junior manager's career. The mentor should work closely with the human resources director and other senior managers so that the individual being mentored has a career path that prepares them for a more senior role as soon as is practical.

Taking oversight of a junior manager's career means more than just advising on and arranging career moves within the company – it can and should mean that, if the person is fundamentally unsuited to the corporate culture, the mentor should advise a move to another company. This is generally in the best interests of the individual and the company as it avoids a mismatch of talent and/or approach. If this is necessary then the mentor should also assist the person in preparing a curriculum vitae and practising for interviews.

Impartiality

The mentor must remain impartial, keeping their responsibilities towards both the company and the individual in balance. They must defend the manager if that person is being unfairly criticised but must accept the criticism if fair and just and in the company's best interests. This can be very difficult and can put considerable pressure on the mentor, who must remain a disinterested observer.

Impartiality is easier to maintain if the mentor remembers that the role is to ensure that their 'godson' or 'goddaughter' needs to be developed so that they add value to the company. The mentor is not there as the person's manager and any criticism of the person is not a criticism of the mentor – it is, however, an opportunity to assist the development of the company and its people.

One very difficult aspect of having to maintain impartiality is what to do when it is clear that the manager being mentored is failing to achieve the performance expected. This comes back to the fundamental problem of investment return – the company must make a return on its investment in its people – and there is a limit to how much effort can realistically be made to develop an individual. If a fair effort has been made then the mentor should consider the company first and the manager second and should assist that manager in finding another post – either in a different division or with another company.

Performance appraisals

It is vital that a mentoring programme involves the mentor in the performance appraisal of those that they mentor.

Performance appraisals – those annual events that determine the future training requirements, career opportunities and financial rewards – are human resource management activities that are normally the direct responsibility of the immediate superior. This can present all sorts of problems, not the least of which is that a manager may not actually enjoy a good relationship with their superior. Other problems can also exist – in today's diverse and globally dispersed companies it is quite likely that a person's superior is not based in the same geographical location, which can make it difficult to achieve a fair appraisal of performance. This is especially true if anything other than hard goals, such as sales volumes and financial returns, are included.

The mentor is in a position to provide an impartial contribution to the appraisal, especially in terms of the developmental needs of the individual. They are also able to provide feedback on the improvements in the soft skills that have been achieved during the past year. When combined with the results of the numerical goals that most managers have, this additional input provides a complete picture that allows a proper and unbiased appraisal to be conducted.

It is important, of course, that the manager concerned fully understands that their mentor will make a contribution to their appraisal; but they must also be assured that the input will be confined to their developmental achievements and future needs and will have no impact on how their other goals are assessed.

Reassignment

Finally, the mentor should also view mentoring as an opportunity to get the right people in the right jobs. A functional head may well view their team only in terms of the activities of the department, whereas the mentor, being outside the department, will be able to asssess whether a manager would be better suited to a position in another team. This is an area in which impartial judgement of what is best for the company and the individual will allow recommendations for reassignment to be made even if this produces a temporary 'problem' for a department.

Department heads are reluctant to suggest that a manager should join another team or department except in cases in which they wish to get rid of the person. This is a common human reaction − if the team works well, the team leader will not want to lose a member even when this is in the best interests of the company. Team leaders are, naturally, primarily interested in what is best for their team and taking the wider view is frequently not in their short-term interests.

In setting up a mentoring programme, you may like to consider making the mentor's input a precondition to any reassignment. In this way, the mentor can act as a 'check and balance' on managers who would prefer to move a person out of a team rather than make any effort to develop and help them succeed.

Responsibilities of the person being mentored

Responsibility to the company

With most training and development programmes there is a great deal of emphasis on the responsibilities of the programme and the people delivering it; but the person receiving or benefiting from the programme also has responsibilities and this is particularly true in mentoring.

In exchange for the pay received, people contract with a company or organisation to provide professionally delivered intellectual or physical work; the more they are paid, the greater the value of work they must deliver. Development programmes, such as mentoring, equip people to provide *added value* to their work and the more effort made by the company to develop their skills and abilities, the greater the added value they must deliver. It is their responsibility, as the recipients of mentoring, to deliver an increased performance and added value *without expecting to receive an increase in pay*. An increase in pay comes with an increase in work-related responsibilities. While not suggesting that companies should refrain from rewarding enhanced performance, it is necessary to stress that enhanced performance does not bestow a *right* to additional pay.

Responsibility to the mentor

Mentoring is not a one-way responsibility. While the mentor takes responsibility for the development of the individual, the individual must take responsibility for their own participation in the mentoring programme.

Mentors, being senior managers, are busy people and their time is far more valuable to the company than that of the junior manager; so it falls to the individual to cooperate and coordinate with the mentor. For example, when the mentor requests or suggests a meeting, the individual must select a convenient time and must protect the appointment.

Since the mentor is making a scarce resource (their time) available, the individual must respect this and make good use of it. Wasting a mentor's time by not being ready, by not getting to the point, or by being solely concerned with their own agenda, are all ways in which the individual shows disrespect for their mentor.

Responsibility to themselves

In addition to their responsibility towards the company and the mentor, the individual must also demonstrate responsibility towards themselves. This means that they must actively involve themselves in the development programme and make as full a use as possible of their mentor. To fail to take advantage of the mentoring programme is a rejection of the efforts being made by the company and by the mentor, and can lead to the conclusion that the individual does not wish to enhance their own performance. While this is obviously a demonstration of a lack of responsibility towards the company, it also demonstrates a lack of responsibility towards their own personal development.

CHAPTER NINE

Structuring a mentoring programme

A properly structured mentoring programme is well worth the effort in terms of both investment and return but it does have to be remembered that, like a coaching programme, mentoring is not a free activity. Depending entirely on how the programme is put together and what its objectives are, mentoring can range from the inexpensive to the very expensive – especially if your company is globally diverse.

Structuring the programme is not difficult but it does require some step-by-step development and implementation.

THE MENTORING PROGRAMME

1   What are the objectives?

2   Developing the programme

- ■ Who will mentor?
- ■ Who will be mentored?
- ■ Mentoring commitment: time involved
- ■ Reports and action plans
- ■ Investment return

3   Implementing the programme

4   Monitoring

5   Review and modification

1 What are the objectives?

At its most simple, the programme's objective is obviously 'improving the performance of managers'. Given the need for investment return, however, it may be better if certain objectives are properly conceived. A good place to start is with a mission statement:

> To develop the productivity and effectiveness of the managers in the company so that the entire performance of the company is enhanced by 10% when measured by the performance of each department against its annual goals.

Whatever you choose as your overall objective, it must include a stated improvement in performance and a method of measuring it. This is very important if an investment return is to be achieved.

Once you have decided on the overall objective, you can prepare the individual goals for different parts of the programme, and its development and implementation. This is also important as it takes time to complete each step and measurable results may not be observable, or achievable, for some time – however, senior management will want to know how the process is doing and whether goals are being achieved long before a measurable improvement in the performance of the company is apparent.

Typically, you should set a timeframe for:

- the complete development of the programme

- selecting the mentors and their training

- selection of participants and their allocation to mentors

- the setting of achievable and believable goals for each mentoring relationship

■   monitoring the performance of the
     programme.

2 Developing the programme

Any programme that is going to deliver a 'profit' to the
company in terms of enhanced performance has to be carefully prepared and costed. A considerable amount of work is
involved in the initial development of a mentoring
programme and the short-term gain may not appear worthwhile – but mentoring is a *long-term* project and it is the
long-term return to the company that must be the deciding
criteria.

You should carefully plan both the programme itself and
how it should be implemented. This plan should be written
down so that it can be referred to and modified as necessary.
The plan becomes the operating 'manual' for the
programme and can be used by everyone to see what is
happening and what results are expected.

After preparing the first draft, senior management
should meet, as it is vital to get everyone fully committed –
especially as senior managers are likely to be the
principal mentors. At the meeting you should present the
draft plan and then give all senior managers a copy with
the objective of obtaining their input to improve the
programme. This will also strengthen their commitment, as
people are much more willing to support a programme they
have contributed towards than one that is imposed. And by
the whole process you are keeping them informed and thus
interested.

At this stage, you might choose to withhold your
thoughts on what the goals of the programme should be,
and you should be reluctant to state the final budget
although you could offer some general figures. If you do
have to present budget ideas at this stage then you should
also present some investment returns.

When the final version of the plan has been prepared you should again circulate it, with goals and budget, but this time make clear that a final discussion and sign-off will take place at a pre-planned meeting. It is better to get the item slotted into a management meeting rather than call a separate meeting as this would suggest that the programme is a 'fact' rather than still a subject for discussion.

Who will mentor?

As discussed in the previous chapter, it is the senior managers who will be delivering the mentoring but it is necesary to outline exactly which people are to be involved.

Unless short of mentors, the company should avoid asking the Chief Executive or Managing Director to become a mentor as this can prove to be a responsibility for which they do not have the capacity. It is also a problem for those managers being mentored – one way or another, everyone reports ultimately to the CEO or MD of the company and it is best that no manager has a mentoring relationship with someone in the same reporting line.

All other senior managers should be asked to be mentors. To build commitment, you should ensure that the senior managers are all in the plan by name and function rather than just noted as 'all senior managers'.

Who will be mentored?

As discussed in the previous chapter, various selection criteria can be used to choose the managers who are to be mentored and, while these must be the guide, the ultimate criterion must be the number of potential managers to be mentored and the number of mentors available. The reasoning is simple: capacity will determine the number actually involved and this will dictate the other selection criteria.

Experience suggests that senior managers are only happy

with mentoring if the process does not take up too much of their time. Quite what is 'too much' is open to debate, but most senior managers should be asked to mentor no more than four 'godchildren'. On this basis, the number of junior managers involved in the programme is calculated as being four times the number of mentors available. With this capacity restriction in place, other selection criteria, such as fast-track, can be applied.

Be warned: some senior managers may not be willing to mentor as many as four 'godchildren' and this will also have to be taken into account. However, four is a good number to work with. Other than the reluctance of senior managers to take on too much, the reasons for selecting four as a maximum are:

- senior managers still have to coach, develop and lead their own team

- four 'godchildren' is a practical number in the light of the mentoring commitment involved in a successful programme.

Once you have calculated the number of junior managers who can be mentored, and you have selected them, you must then allocate them to the available mentors. This should be done specifically by name and function and recorded down in the plan. In this way you can ensure that nobody is in a mentoring relationship with someone in the same reporting line and that all parties know exactly who is involved with whom.

Mentoring commitment: time involved

Mentors should meet formally with each of their 'godchildren' once each quarter − although twice a year may be a practical minimum in some companies − and these mentoring meetings should be for as long as is necessary for the mentor to carry out their responsibilities. This could be anything from half a day to a day. Of course, mentors may choose to meet with their 'godchildren' more frequently if this is necessary and many will meet anyway in the course of business, but the formal mentoring meetings need to be protected. In addition to face-to-face meetings, the mentor will also need to be in touch with his 'godchild' on a regular basis by telephone or e-mail.

Assuming you have established four meetings per year as a minimum, then with four 'godchildren' each mentor will be involved in 16 days' mentoring per year as a minimum. In an average working year of 220 days, this represents 7.5% of their available time. When combined with the necessary information-gathering, follow-up, reports, and action plans, this could easily double to 15% of their time. To put this further into perspective, this is eight working days or approximately two working weeks each quarter. And there are not many senior managers who will be able or willing to find more than this amount of time.

Even eight days per 'godchild' per year may appear an underestimate when you start to add in the time taken on contributing towards appraisals (probably another half day per person) and to career development meetings with other senior managers (another half day per person). It is possible, therefore, that a conscientious mentor will devote up to nine days per year per 'godchild' – if they have four 'godchildren' this represents 36 working days a year, very close to 20% of their available time.

And the commitment of the mentor goes beyond just time – they must ensure that their 'godchildren' are receiving the necessary development assistance as outlined in earlier chapters.

On the other side of the relationship, the 'godchild' also has commitments to the programme that must be spelled out in the plan. In the first place, their commitment is to attending the requisite number of meetings each year – and they should take a proactive approach to ensuring that the mentoring meetings take place: junior managers must take some responsibility for their own development and must not rely on others to make all the arrangements.

In addition, the junior manager must then carry out the action plans and make sure that they receive the development coaching and training that has been agreed. They must also provide regular monthly reporting to their mentor on what has been achieved. These reports need not be more than a few sentences long, depending on the actions planned for that month, but they have to be prepared and sent and this takes a little time.

Reports and action plans

Beyond the monthly reporting of those being mentored, additional reporting is necessary if you are going to be able to monitor the performance of the programme, vital for you to determine the investment return.

The data you need will have to be acquired from various sources:

- volume data such as sales, revenue, costs, and so on, from the company MIS system

- the performance monitoring of the individual teams – for performance against their team and individual goals

- the training records – for data on what training and development work has been carried out including coaching

- the annual appraisals, available from the human resources department

- the mentors' quarterly and annual reports on their 'godchildren' plus the action plans that have been developed and implemented

■ data on the cost of the programme against budget, from the financial control systems.

Certain reportings can be specified in the plan while others will have to be outlined; listing them all ensures that all management can see where you intend to acquire the information and what their commitments are for providing data and reports. You will also need to determine the frequency of all reports as this will determine the frequency of your reporting on the performance of the programme. On this latter point, you should arrange for your initial report to be delivered after three months, followed by a second report after a further three months – thereafter your reporting should be at six-monthly intervals. Each year, of course, you should provide a report on cost and investment return so that senior management can see the benefit of the programme in financial terms.

Investment return

Mentoring is a company activity and must be carried out in company time and at the company's expense.

This rather self-evident statement carries significant budgetary implications. Consider a small company that is located in one place. Beyond the use of mentoring time, there is little in the way of extra expense – no one has to spend time and money on travel, no one has to use external phone lines or the postal system: mentor and 'godchild' are 'just down the hall from each other', so to speak. But when we consider a large company that is geographically spread out, the picture is very different and the budget implications are greater. The most significant costs, other than the time involved, will be that of travel and the telephone as the mentors keep in touch with those they are mentoring.

Estimating the investment returns of the programme is unlikely to be an exact science. However, improving the performance of managers is so that they improve the performance of their teams. So we can generally look at the team performance and then attach some financial figures to it.

As with coaching programmes, mentoring should produce a measurable improvement of around 10% per annum in performance terms and this figure should be used to show the potential investment return. If it is achieved, then the return on the programme should be significantly above the cost, thus providing a clear 'profit' to the company.

3 Implementing the programme

The plan should show the implementation phases in a clear and logical manner and provide an explanation of how the programme will be put in place, along with a clear timetable. Remember, this is a new programme so it must be communicated clearly to everyone. Once the programme is up and running, new entrants can simply be assigned to a mentor and provided with a summary of the programme requirements.

So what are the steps for implementation?

(a) Communication of the programme

There are three steps you should take to communicate the programme to all concerned:

(i) a memorandum to all mentors outlining the programme and whom they will be mentoring
(ii) a memorandum to each of the managers selected for the programme outlining the programme and explaining who will be their mentor
(iii) a meeting of all managers and mentors involved in the programme so that the inevitable questions can be answered and everyone gets an opportunity to see who is involved.

The memoranda are basically the same. You should give

an overview of what mentoring is about, why it is being implemented, and what the expected results should be. You should then give a more detailed breakdown of the commitments that will have to be made and the responsibilities of both the mentor and the person being mentored. This should include such things as the number of meetings that will take place, the reports and action plans that will be developed, and by whom; and who will be responsible for the overall coordination and control of the programme.

The mentors should be told who their 'godchildren' are, along with their functions, who their direct superiors are, the contact address and phone numbers of the individuals and their superiors. You also enclose a complete list of who is being mentored (by name and function) and by whom. This enables the mentors to keep track of the relationships. Managers being mentored must be told who their mentor is and be provided with a contact address and telephone number.

The coordinator should provide their name and contact information, although it may be better if the memoranda are sent out over the signature of the MD or CEO as this provides additional evidence of the commitment of the company to the process and shows that it is a programme that is eventually reported to the CEO or MD.

The meeting should take place before the official commencement date of the programme. You should also arrange for the CEO or MD to attend and to outline the programme and its benefits. If at all possible, you should hold just one meeting for everyone; however, if your company is very geographically dispersed it may be necessary to hold a series of meetings pulling together those managers and mentors in each particular location.

The meeting should follow this format:

(i) Welcome by the programme coordinator, to explain the purpose of the meeting and the agenda.
(ii) Introduction to the programme by the CEO or MD.

(iii) Question-and-Answer session chaired by the coordinator.
(iv) Group meetings between the mentors and their 'god-children' – this is necessary as many of the managers will not have met their mentors before and it is an opportunity to break the ice and for the mentors to set up the initial meetings.

(b) Follow-up communications

The second part of the implementation is to send out a short reminder communication towards the end of the first quarter to request feedback from the mentors on how their initial meetings went and to review the action plans that were established.

4 Monitoring

It is absolutely essential that the performance of the mentoring programme is monitored but this is often the one step that is not carried out properly. If monitoring is not done then the actual application of the programme tends to be spasmodic and the whole thing fails to deliver all the benefits. Monitoring is as much to do with measurement of performance as it is to ensure that all parties in the programme are fulfilling their responsibilities.

As a minimum, you will need to keep records of the numbers of mentoring meetings that take place in each relationship, the actions that were planned, and their outcome. In addition, you will almost certainly have to check that the mentors are making an input to the annual appraisals.

Monitoring and measuring the performance enhancement of the individuals as a result of the programme is also a vital area as this is where the real benefits to the company occur. It is also where you will be able to determine the investment return. What is to be measured and how was discussed earlier and you can also use the monitoring of the coaching programme as an additional source of information (although don't make the mistake of attributing the results of coaching to the mentoring programme). Remember, the success of the programme is based on the investment return and enhanced performance *as it is measured and reported to senior management*. There may well be other benefits but success is judged by senior management on their terms – which are objective and based on data.

5 Review and modification

As with all plans, you should establish a periodic review process so that the programme itself can be enhanced through modification. Your initial plan should include an outline of this review process and should also define the areas that may be subject to modification – for example, the criteria for selecting participants or mentors.

PART FOUR: DEVELOPING MANAGERS

Enabling key people to deliver the leadership the organisation requires

Many large companies spent much of the 1980s and 1990s altering their management structures so as to get rid of supposedly excess managers. Those same companies are now finding that they have lost a key group of people on whose knowledge, dedication, and ability the company depended. What is done is done – but we can learn from the mistakes of others.

If we have the right people in the right jobs, then we will also have the right managers in the right places to lead them and to manage the company's business processes. And these managers need development – development that goes beyond routine training and coaching – since it is on its managers that the future success of a company depends.

Managers, and especially senior managers, are a special group when it comes to planning their development. The company that develops and retains its best managers is the company that will succeed in its chosen field.

In the following chapter we will be looking at:

- Management and leadership
- What needs to be developed
- Who will coach the managers
- Setting up a management coaching programme
- Solutions for developing senior managers

CHAPTER TEN

Managers – a developmental imperative

Perhaps one of the most important assignments you can have is the development of managers. Managers, by the nature of their position, are often thought to be beyond the need of development and this is especially true with the more senior managers. Managers, themselves, fall into the same trap and believe they do not need further training or coaching.

The truth is, however, that managers, *perhaps more than anyone else*, would benefit from training, coaching and other developmental activity. The performance of a manager is vital to the success of the team, and the success of the organisation, and this is especially true of front-line managers. If those who seek to lead the people in *value-generating* roles are not *adding value* themselves through proper leadership, then the team will not be maximising the value that they generate for the company. This must be addressed as a matter of urgency.

Management vs. leadership

The big problem for most managers is that is what they are – *managers*. They are not *leaders*, except in the nominal sense of the word, and their role is to focus on the short-term results of the process. Deal and Kennedy, in their book *Corporate Cultures: The Rites and Rituals of Corporate Life* (Addison Wesley), studied managers and leaders; other researchers have made similar studies, and some of the differences found between managers and leaders are listed below:

Managers

- Process-oriented
- Planned view of their work unit
- Rational decision-making based on plan
- Always busy and have little time for unscheduled interruptions
- Routine-driven and inflexible in response to pressure
- Concerned about the details and short-term results, focused on 'the numbers'
- Are uncomfortable unless there is order

Leaders

- Task-focused
- Vision of the team and its goals
- Intuitive decision-making based on vision
- Always make time available – an opportunity may result
- Willing to experiment and respond flexibly to new challenges
- Concerned about details in terms of the overall scheme and achieving the long-term task
- Thrive on chaos

A company needs both

Every organisation needs both managers and leaders if it is to succeed. It needs people who will focus on the short-term objectives of making the process work efficiently and effectively and others to focus on the long-term strategic goals. This mistake occurs when the organisation expects managers to take on leadership responsibilities – although both functions are task-focused, the range of that focus is different.

A leader must know and understand the full objective of their team whereas the manager needs only to know the objective of the process for which they are responsible – they may not even know (or need to know) how the objective of the process fits with the overall objectives envisioned by the leader. Managers, in other words, fulfil a necessary supervisory role that is purely *tactical*. The leader, on the other hand, must act *strategically* to achieve the organisation's objectives.

Many senior managers look around them and see so much inferior management that they believe they would be better off with less management and a much flatter organisation, but this could be a fallacy. As Thomas Teal said in his 1996 book, *First Person: Tales of Management Courage and*

Tenacity: '... think, for a moment, what the world was like before the principles of *scientific management* led to huge leaps forward in technology, the rationalisation of production, the democratisation of wealth, the development of advanced scientific study resulting in readily available medicines and modern technology, and the effective doubling of life expectancy'. Good management works miracles – and all companies could benefit.

Are expectations too high?

So why is there so much mediocre management? Why do managers fail to obtain the best performance from their people? Why are many senior managers failing as leaders?

The answer lies in what is expected of managers in today's business environment and how they are prepared for the role they are expected to play. In a traditional management role – say, one up from a team supervisor – they are expected to have a range of traditional 'management' skills in such areas as:

Finance	Financial control
Budgeting	Cost control
Resource allocation	Product development
Marketing	Manufacturing
Operations	Technology

This list is by no means definitive – there are literally dozens of other skills we expect the manager to have.

Then there are the less distinct skills, or management 'arts', and managers are expected to perform at a high level in:

Strategic planning	Tactical planning
Presenting	Persuading
Negotiating	Writing
Speaking	Listening

Again, this list is not definitive.

And once a manager is found with all these skills they are then expected to display leadership characteristics, such as:

Integrity	Ethical standards
Honesty	Vision
Strength of purpose	Passion
Commitment	Sensitivity
Task focus	Team focus
Individual focus	Individuality
Team membership	Luck
Courage	Humility
Charisma	Motivation
Tenacity	Self-confidence

And when they've displayed all this, they are expected to subjugate their personal interests and ambition to the greater good of the company, to work long hours and to look out for the best interests of the organisation.

The key element

There is, however, one key element missing from the lists above: *people-management*: the ability to manage and lead people so that they will deliver the performance that the organisation requires so that it can reach its goals. People-management, above all else, is what management and leadership is about and without the necessary ability in this area, no matter how skilled they are in other fields, the manager is next to worthless to the organisation – they will not *add value* in their role.

A lack of professional training

Management has become one of the most common jobs in the late twentieth century – at sometime or another just about everyone is asked to be a manager and they are expected to have all, and more, of the skills, arts, and characteristics listed above. The problem is that no one seems to have considered the training of these people in realistic terms.

Consider for a moment: you are ill and in need of medical attention. Would you (a) see a non-qualified doctor – a 'quack', or (b) go to a properly trained and qualified doctor? When you get on an aeroplane do you prefer (a) a pilot who has never learned to fly, or (b) a properly trained and qualified pilot? The answers are self-evident and yet, when it comes to running a business, companies quite calmly *assume* that the managers they select are capable of doing the job. Managing a company is one of the few professional occupations in which training and a professional qualification are not considered necessary – indeed, many top business leaders are even proud of the fact that they have no formal qualifications.

Although being a manager is a very common occupation, only a small proportion of those doing the job have actually set out to be managers – most have joined the company to do a specific job and have found themselves in management roles, generally by accident and frequently without any training whatsoever. Those who have chosen management as a career can get qualifications and many colleges of technology and some universities offer business administration and management studies at pre-degree and first-degree level; and, of course, there are business schools within many universities that are now offering postgraduate MBA degrees. All the courses focus on the hard skills of management in combination with the planning parts of the management arts. But, just about no degree course attempts to teach students about the soft skills of people-management and leadership. For those who wish to obtain a professional qualification the management sciences are well catered for but we are still in the Dark Ages as far as teaching the management and leadership of people is concerned.

A problem ignored

As a result of this imbalance between management sciences and people-management, there is a tendency in many companies to downplay the importance of leadership, of managing people for performance. Unfortunately, learning how to lead people while, at the same time, trying to deliver the company's goals all too often results in a failure to deliver either. Yet the average company makes little or no effort to address this issue.

It is entirely possible that the root cause of the problem is senior management's own lack of formal training in leadership and people-management, which results in their having a high level of fear at the thought of offering coaching to others on this subject. This fear is mainly based on the fact that they suspect that their own leadership skills are not that good.

But it goes further. Senior management are also reluctant to offer coaching on the hard skills or the management arts since they assume that those in management have already reached the necessary level and do not need further development. This poses the question: if experienced line workers can benefit from training and coaching to improve their performance, wouldn't experienced managers benefit similarly?

Since it is a given that everyone can benefit and have their performance enhanced through coaching, it follows that all managers can also benefit from coaching. The problems are: what needs to be coached, who will do the coaching and how do you set up the programme?

What needs to be developed?

Refreshing hard skills

The hard skills needed by managers, along with the more ephemeral skills of strategic planning and so on, are often very technical – many even have individual professional qualifications attached. For example, financial control functions often require a full accountancy training and qualification, production management can be studied at university or with a professional institute, marketing can be studied at various well-respected marketing institutes and the role of a Director in the UK can be studied with the Insititute of Directors.

This means that the senior managers in such roles are, in general, technically well qualified in the hard skills needed for them to do their jobs. If their performance should decline, however, it is unlikely that the company has anyone who can coach them – except, perhaps, the functional head, but this person is probably far too busy to be able to spend adequate time with junior managers coaching them on technical skills. In the circumstances, it would probably be wise to make use of the external training courses available through the various professional institutes and to have all managers attend technical refresher courses on a regular basis so that they are up-to-date on the latest techniques and skills in their chosen field.

Developing soft skills

On the other hand, the soft skills – the people-management and leadership skills – must often be developed from scratch. The first step is to ensure that all managers, from the most junior to the most senior, have attended a basic workshop on managing people, or leadership. Such a workshop should look at:

- the role of the leader and the role of the follower

- motivation

- performance-management skills

- personal management and leadership profiles

- team-building, including team decision-making and maximising the performance of teams.

Most such workshops run for one week with follow-up one-day events to ensure the skills have been learned. Providing these courses are run by a credible and recognised expert from outside the organisation, participants will gain a good understanding of the soft management skills necessary and will be able to practise them in a non-threatening environment.

The skills learned on this sort of management workshop can be coached in the work environment and should form part of the main coaching programme. The other soft skills, such as communication or interpersonal relationships, are far more difficult to teach in a training seminar and improving performance in these is best handled by the coach. The issue that arises is that people frequently respond in a defensive or negative manner when offered advice and coaching on such personal topics. While senior managers are less likely to *show* such behaviour than are more junior ones, they are, nevertheless, just as defensive and coaching such people can be very difficult.

But coach them you must. Management of people in the modern organisation is based on a series of interpersonal interactions and the more senior the manager the more likely they are to spend their days interacting with people rather than on the technical aspects of their job – after all, they have more junior managers and teams to do that for them.

Delegation

Nearly thirty years ago Lawrence Peter (in *The Peter Principle*, 1969) suggested that workers in general, and managers in particular, get promoted to one position beyond that which they are competent to fulfil, and this results either in their being ineffective or persisting in doing the job of the person below them.

This is the first thing that has to be addressed – you need to coach the manager on what *they* are supposed to be doing and you need to show them ways of stepping away from doing what *their subordinates* should be doing. This goes beyond the straightforward teaching of delegation skills and is more a case of confidence-building as they come to terms with what their role demands of them – the things for which only they are responsible and which can only be done by the person in their role. Of course, learning to delegate is one part of this but much more important is learning to let go of those things that *should* be done – rather than could be done – by others.

Understanding what can only be done by the manager and what should be done by others requires an analysis of all the principal aspects of the manager's job. This should be done in terms of three categories:

1 what must be done by the manager
2 what must be delegated to others
3 what can be delegated to others if they have the capacity and capability to handle it.

Analysis would suggest that:

1 *Only the manager can*:

■ set the overall objectives for the team

■ help each individual set their own goals

■ monitor the team objectives to ensure they are achieved

■ take responsibility for the team goals

■ plan and allocate the work to ensure that everyone is 'pulling their weight'

- obtain and allocate the resources for the team

- oversee the development of, and to coach, the team.

2 *The manager MUST delegate to the team*:

- the authority to do their work in a way that will achieve their goals

- all the activities that are part of their jobs.

3 *If the team has the capacity and capability, the manager may be able to delegate*:

- the monitoring of the team members' own goals

- the authority to make decisions and inform the manager only after the event

Once the manager is fully familiar with this sort of analysis you can then look at their delegation skills and coach them accordingly. Delegation does not mean that they should just *tell* people to do things: they must understand the team member's development level, be confident that they can carry out the task, and must develop a way of *asking* the team member to carry out the task that leaves the individual feeling confident. This is best done using the delegation model shown.

A manager unused to delegating effectively will need to practise this structure until they are able to use it in a seamless way and with confidence. The important thing is to ensure that all parts are carried out in the correct order and that the final step is a *request*. Most teams in a modern organisation are made up of people with a considerable degree of knowledge and training and these people cannot be treated as if they were unskilled drones – at their level of competence, they must be managed in a participative manner and not through 'command and control'.

A DELEGATION MODEL

1   *Position the discussion*
    Explain what needs to be done by clearly
    stating the situation and the objective

2   *Explain the reason for the delegation*
    Express confidence in the person's ability to
    carry out the task in a satisfactory manner

3   *Explain what needs to be done*
    Unless the task is self-explanatory, explain the
    steps that will have to be carried out, includ-
    ing the timeframe

4   *Request the person take the responsibility*
    Delegate the responsibility by *requesting* that
    the person carry out the task

Participation generally precludes ordering people around in a 'do this' manner – a 'please ensure this is done' approach is much more effective.

Capacity – a major constraint

One problem faced by most managers is that there are many things that can and should be delegated to the team *if the team have the capacity and capability to handle them*: but how to ensure capacity and capability? Managers need coaching on how to understand the developmental needs and develop-mental levels of their team members. They need to accept that it is their direct responsibility to ensure that their team develop the *capability* to carry out tasks that are beyond the narrow confines of their job. But, of course, this does not address the problem of *capacity*.

Capacity is a direct result of the assigned resources. If you have adequate resources then you will have adequate capacity for the work, but if the resources are incorrectly utilised then the capacity they can cope with will be diminished. Maximising capacity is a matter of correct application of skills, correct work flow and good time-management, and it is the manager's responsibility to ensure that the team is doing these things. However, you will probably need to coach the manager in this – many believe their teams are working at maximum capacity and yet, if skills are applied properly and work flow organised correctly, they will find their capacity for work is far greater.

Managers can be coached on how to ensure that the work flow is organised correctly and good time-management applied. They can be coached on getting their team to deliver a high percentage of their capacity, but care must be taken to ensure they also understand that capacity is a double-edged sword. Working at 100% capacity can be as disadvantageous as working at 40% as far as the company is concerned. Ask any production manager in any factory and they will tell you that once you cross the 85% capacity threshold, as an average performance, then problems occur – there is no flexibility to cope with people being absent, for machinery to be maintained, for things to be corrected if they go wrong – and the stress of working at near 100% capacity can increase the number of days lost to sickness. The same thing applies in most other teams and you should aim to have an 80% to 85% capacity utilisation as your goal rather than going for 100%.

Who will coach the managers?

It seems to be a very human reaction that advice is only acceptable from someone 'older and wiser'. Mature managers in their forties and fifties are, therefore, unlikely to take kindly to coaching from a person in their twenties or thirties, no matter how experienced or expert that person may be. The real problem is, therefore, who coaches mature managers?

It should be possible for the assistance of a good coach to be accepted by any manager, no matter how mature or senior they are in relation to the coach. The reality is different and the situation needs to be addressed very carefully. One solution is to present the coaching in people-management as development of a *technical* skill – this makes it possible to establish the coach as a person with credibility as a people-manager or an expert in industrial or business psychology and communications. Such people, recruited specifically to act in the management-development role, would be experienced and effective people-managers or professionally trained industrial and business psychologists, who would focus entirely on enhancing the skills of active managers.

It may be a radical concept, but it would be worth considering recruiting senior managers who have retired from an active and successful management career and who would welcome the chance to make available their experience as leaders. These management coaches would probably work part-time on a regular programme of meetings with mature and senior managers so as to help them develop – or enhance their performance in people-management skills.

Another source of such coaches is your own organisation – in the downsizing and de-layering of companies that is still going on, there will be a range of experienced managers whose jobs are now redundant, or those who would welcome the opportunity to work part-time before taking full retirement. The added advantage is that such managers would bring to the role a wealth of company-related experience that an outsider would take years to acquire.

If these approaches are not available to you then your source of management coaches will have to be found within the current management structure – something that many companies will find very difficult.

Setting up a management coaching programme

Managers are very busy people – they work long hours and often tell you that they do not have time to get everything done during the normal working day. Putting aside the training opportunity that this statement conjures up, it highlights one of the problems associated with setting up a management coaching programme – managers are busy and coaching them must not further add to their commitments.

In reality, managers are often reluctant to receive training and coaching as they feel it may well show up their own failings and limitations. So how can you set up an acceptable management coaching programme?

Since management coaching needs to focus on the soft skills of people-management and leadership, the programme should be based on the coach in the role of unbiased observer (as presented in chapter six) – an observer who does not participate in the events but comments and advises in private, and provides alternative methods of handling situations. If the right people have been selected for this sensitive role, then the relationship between the manager and coach is likely to become one of leader and trusted advisor, with the coach being allowed to work more and more closely with the manager to ensure that the latter's people-management skills are enhanced as much as possible.

As with any coaching programme, it should not be sprung as a surprise as this generates resentment and resistance. Instead, the programme should be announced at a meeting of all managers and the selected coaches introduced. Then the programme should be implemented with the coaches spending a set number of days with each manager over a period of time. During these days, the coach should accompany the manager during all their business activities and then follow up each one by engaging in a review of what was done well and what could have been handled better. The coach can then offer advice on how to improve. In many ways a management coaching programme is closer to a mentoring programme than it is to the type of coaching programme outlined in Part Two.

Solutions for developing senior managers

Who should train, coach or mentor senior managers?

Training for senior managers

Subject knowledge

Let us go back to the point made earlier in this chapter – that the technical training of senior managers should be left to specialist courses run by training companies and professional institutes as the level of knowledge available within the company is likely to be less than that of the senior managers needing training. From this point of view, it may be wise for the development programme for a senior manager to include a regular refresher course in their technical subject or, as a minimum, attendance at a variety of specialist short conferences within their subject field.

There are literally thousands of useful conferences of this type being run through the year. Sometimes they make use of speakers who are practitioners in the field or are well-known managers themselves, sometimes the speakers are consultants or academics, but the common theme is always that recognised authorities are called in to address the delegates on specific subjects that are topical, important, and need considering by professionals.

Executive development courses

Another source of training for senior managers is the short courses run by various business schools within the university sector. These courses, generally referred to as Executive Development Programmes, run for anything from four weeks to six months and are held on the university campus.

The curriculum for the courses varies according to the specialisation of the speakers, lecturers and professors available but, typically, covers strategy, marketing, human resource planning and utilisation, business modelling, financial management, macro-economics, and sector-specific subjects such as banking, capital markets, governmental policies, and foreign trade. In many cases, the format of the course closely resembles the MBA course run by the university and the teaching may include case-studies, lectures, syndicate work, individual projects, and projects specific to the delegates' own companies.

These mini MBA courses and Executive Development Programmes are both popular and very valuable as they allow senior managers to step away from their day-to-day issues and to reflect on and rebuild their knowledge of business while in an academic environment. The downside is that small companies often cannot allow a senior manager to be away for such an extended period of time. In these circumstances, they will have to search for such courses that run on a part-time basis or are split up into small components spread over a longer period or are structured for distance learning.

Mentoring

A mentoring programme is probably the only solution to the development of senior managers once you are outside the technical skills and into the area of general management arts. Mentoring may, indeed, be the only solution to the problem of developing senior managers who think they are beyond the need of coaching, or are afraid that their weaknesses will be exposed if they submit to a development programme. There is some sense behind their apprehension – if a senior manager has, as his trainer or coach, a more junior person *from within the company* or even a colleague, then there is certainly a risk that the senior manager's authority will be damaged, and this would be damaging to the company. On the other hand, everyone is able to improve their performance. So here the approach is different to the mentoring programme you will have set up for the rest of the management structure – you will no longer be able to use mentors from inside the organisation and will have to turn to external mentors.

Selection of external mentors

If you are going to bring in an outsider to advise and mentor at very senior levels there is a considerable risk of conflict of interest, especially if the outsider is currently working in business. This is not, however, as big a problem as some people choose to imagine – after all, it is exactly the same principle as bringing in a non-executive director. The main difference between the two is that a non-executive director is there to act as a check and balance to the executive directors while contributing towards the overall good governance of the company. The external mentor, on the other hand, is there to develop the skills of the senior manager and not to make any specific contribution towards the running of the company.

Senior managers may well already have a mentor – someone they have known for some time and whose opinions they respect – but it is unlikely they will have entered into a formal mentoring relationship. To bring in the right sort of mentor and to establish a proper mentoring relationship you will need to recruit, and the first step is to write a job description.

A short case-study illustrates this process well:

The managing director of a small company specialising in the production of multi-media visual aids had four other directors on the board who had day-to-day management responsibilities. When they decided to establish a senior management mentoring programme they set about it as though they were recruiting a non-executive director.

Their first criterion was that they did not want a person from the same industry (this was to avoid conflicts of interest in a highly competitive market). Their second criterion was that the mentor should be old enough to command respect but young enough to fit in with the team. This meant they were looking for someone in their late forties as the average age of the directors was forty-one. Their third criterion was that the mentor had to have extensive hands-on management experience and had to be recognised as a 'good people-manager'. Finally, they wanted someone who could mentor all five directors on a minimum of a four-meetings-per-year basis. As the group comprised two women and three men, they felt there was little reason to opt for a man or a woman although all had a slight preference for a man.

Having agreed these general selection criteria they realised they were looking for someone who (i) wished to become an independent consultant, or (ii) was already a consultant, having held a senior management position, or (iii) was currently a senior manager or director in another company. At this point they sought advice from a recruitment consultancy and decided that they would look for somone who wanted a career change involving part-time work. They also determined the sort of salary that they would need to pay.

After careful selection the executive search people were able to offer three candidates for consideration. The first was a man in his mid-fifties who held a number of non-executive directorships and had had a career as senior manager and then director within the sales and marketing side of the automotive industry. The second was an extremely well-known business-man now acting as a consultant and the third was a woman who had spent many years in the computer industry and was now looking for a career move so that she could spend more time with her young family.

Having interviewed each of the candidates, the directors, much to their own surprise, offered the job to the woman from the computer industry, reasoning that (a) their business had similarities in culture to the computer industry, (b) the woman was willing and able to spend the necessary time with the company, and (c) she was a natural team player, a good listener and had no interest in trying to run the company.

The reasoning behind the selection made excellent sense. The similarity of the culture was important – the company was young, dynamic, and in an industry where you are only as good as the last project you completed. The people were very active and committed and there was an open-door policy among the directors – very similar to the smaller computer companies that now exist. The candidate's willingness and ability to spend the 20 to 40 days per year that was necessary was an obvious positive but it was her ability to listen well and to be a team player that was so important. Since she would be mentoring all the directors, she would also become a natural team coach and mentor which would give her significant influence with the management team, and her disinclination to become involved in the running of the company meant that the mentoring rela-tionship would be protected.

The key things that are so important in selecting external mentors are the preparation of a detailed job description complete with responsibilities and how performance will be measured, the ability of the mentors to fit in with the corporate culture, and their need to be disinterested and impartial observers and listeners who will offer non-partisan advice. It is also necessary to follow a 'recruitment' approach and spend both the time and the money necessary to find the right person for the role.

The role of the external mentor

The role of the external mentor is broadly the same as that of the mentors within the company although it is unlikely that you would ask them to make any form of contribution to the annual appraisals of the people being mentored. However, the same responsibilities exist and that includes the reporting and action planning aspects – although to whom they send their reports is a matter that would have to be resolved.

In the multimedia visual aids company, whose case-study was discussed above, the mentor was asked to prepare reports and action plans as normal and these were then discussed with the individuals concerned. No one other than the mentor and the individual ever saw the reports, although the action plans were discussed during special quarterly meetings of the five directors. This enabled the directors to act as a team to assist each of the individuals, something that was very important and very beneficial to the whole company. It also had the knock-on effect of assisting the directors to become better mentors for their 'godchildren' lower down the company.

Because of the nature of the relationship between an external mentor and a senior manager, the role of the mentor will extend into other areas connected with the manager's professional life. Senior managers, because of their position, often find that they have no one to confide in over their concerns and understandable fears about their work. They are paid to be leaders and to demonstrate leadership, which includes acting as the rock to which all others can cling, or as the captain who must often make decisions as to which course to take with only instinct and experience as a guide. Such a role is lonely if there is no one you can talk to and discuss problems and issues, and receive impartial advice – advice that is in the best interests both of the individual and of the company. The external mentor, therefore, will almost certainly find themself in the position of confessor/confidant(e) and will have to fulfil the unspoken responsibilities of that role. This, of course, will lead to additional benefits for the senior manager and the company.

Additional benefits derived from external mentoring

Confidentiality

Besides the expected benefits of improved performance, the senior manager also acquires the benefit of being able to talk through business problems without fear that they will reach colleagues. And by talking them through they may be able to formulate a better solution. Many managers are 'afraid' to discuss business problems with colleagues because they feel that this shows them up in some way as not being on top of their job. In some competitive cultures this fear may be very soundly based, and if this is the case then talking things through with the mentor is a good solution.

The mentor can also provide a sympathetic ear to the manager's concerns about their own personal and professional development and, indeed, this is one of the mentor's main responsibilities. Many senior managers tend to overlook their own development and it can be down to the mentor to ensure that adequate time is spent each year on developing and enhancing the skills that leaders need. This can range from ensuring the manager attends short seminars on topical subjects, through recommending suitable reading

material, to suggesting attendance on executive development courses. Throughout this process the mentor must
keep in mind what is best for the company at the time and
in the long-term, as well as what is best for the individual.

Career moves

The mentor's role as confessor/confidant(e) becomes somewhat more complex when the senior manager decides it is
time to move on. This is a natural part of the growth of an
individual and should not be suppressed; however, it does
present problems for the mentor in maintaining a balance
between loyalty to the individual and loyalty to the
company. If the next career step is inside the company the
problem is lessened – the mentor can play a significant role
in preparing the ground for the move and in finding
someone to fill the vacated role.

Although some companies may choose to limit input
from an outsider when selecting someone to replace a
senior manager, they could be missing out on some valuable
insights. The mentor will have observed their 'godchild' for
some time and will have a very fair idea of what skills and
attributes are necessary to be successful in the role. This
information should be included in the brief that will guide
the search for a successor – it would even be of benefit to
include the mentor in the interview stage of selection.

The problem is exacerbated, however, if the manager
wishes to take a career step away from the company – the
mentor then faces possible divided loyalties: should they
help the individual or protect the company? To address this
issue, it is necessary to look again at the analogy between a
mentor and a non-executive director. The mentor should be
made aware of the intended move at an early stage but
should keep this information confidential until authorised
to reveal it by the individual. However, along with assisting
the individual to prepare for their job search, interviews and
new position, they should also start a discrete process of

'talent-spotting' within the company to identify potential replacements.

If the company is a large one, the mentor may be able to work with other mentors so that together they can advise on a general shuffling of roles when the time comes. In a small company this is much more difficult. The mentor may be the only one operating and their loyalty to the company will be put under considerable strain. However, the mentor's first loyalty in this case must be to the individual while, *at the same time, protecting the company's position.*

How can this be done? Well, in the majority of cases, it is likely that a potential move will be generated by the senior manager seeing a good career opportunity arise or being approached directly. This means that the process will be relatively short and the decision to move may be made before there is a real opportunity to tell the mentor – this reduces the conflict for the mentor but does mean that they will have to work harder and faster to help fill the gap. If the mentor is informed early, then their talent-spotting will have to start quickly and begin with an assessment of the impact on the company. This they may have to keep under wraps for a while. Some may argue that by doing so the mentor is not acting in the best interests of the company, but this is not the case. By not revealing what they know, the mentor is able to ensure that the company continues to function without the distraction which occurs when people know a change is imminent. At the same time, having protected their relationship with the senior manager through confidentiality, they can ensure that the manager continues to deliver professional work even though they are about to leave.

Dealing with executive stress

Finally, the mentor can bring benefit to the relationship by watching out for signs of executive stress: where the stress and strains of senior management start to inhibit the individuals's ability to cope and so set up physical and emotional problems. Although widely recognised as a serious issue in business, stress is often dismissed as just a 'hazard of the job'; this is extremely short-sighted both for the individual and the company. A person showing signs of stress is highly unlikely to be delivering their best performance, while at the same time they are damaging their health in the longer term. Mentors should be aware of the symptoms of stress and the signs of its likely occurrence and should take active steps to deal with it. Stress itself is a complex subject with a number of medical aspects and it is outside the scope of this book to discuss it. However, there are a number of excellent books on the subject that could help enhance a mentor's knowledge.

PART FIVE: MANAGING FOR PERFORMANCE

Technique for Top-Quality Performance

The development of our staff must be a continuous and continuing activity if we are to achieve the goals we have set for the company.

If we have the right people in the right jobs and with the right managers to lead them, we can set bigger and more demanding goals. In turn, this will require us to develop our people further. But development of people is a process of training, coaching and, where appropriate, mentoring – it does not, strictly speaking, include managing for performance. Managing for performance is about motivation, about team-building, about goals and about recognition and reward – all of which are a manager's responsibility and may well lead to the identification of developmental needs.

Managing for performance is interlinked with the development of our people and it is worthwhile developing an understanding of the techniques involved.

In the following chapter we will be looking briefly at:

■   Team-building

■   Goal-setting

■   Annual appraisals

■   Recognition and reward

■   Promotions

CHAPTER ELEVEN

Key actions for further development

As you seek to improve performance you will need to ensure that your managers, at all levels, are delivering performance management. The skills and techniques for this are set out in detail in my book *Managing for Performance* (Piatkus, 1995). There are a number of techniques for human resource management that come in useful in ensuring that the future development of performance is maintained, that the current position is built on, and that continuous quality improvement occurs.

KEY STRATEGIES OF HUMAN RESOURCE MANAGEMENT FOR FUTURE DEVELOPMENT

- Team-building – ensuring the company has effective teams

- Goal-setting – coordination of tactical and strategic goals

- Annual appraisals – ensuring that developmental needs are met and career paths are properly maintained

- Recognition and reward – acknowledging top-quality performance

- Promotions – who, how and when to promote

Team-building

While it is the direct responsibility of each team leader to ensure that the team is functioning effectively and delivering its goals, teams do need to be developed and this is a training and coaching function.

Ideally, each team should be carefully selected so that the correct skills are matched with personal attributes that allow the team to work together. The primary need, however, is that the right skills are in place and this is addressed through proper selection processes, as already discussed. But once the people have been assigned, there are areas of interaction that can be trained and coached to ensure that the people function as a team.

Communication and decision-making

When successful teams are compared with dysfunctional teams, one of the key findings is that the quality of the communications is better. Successful teams have, deliberately or by luck, achieved clear and effective communication strategies that go beyond the clear use of words. In a team, there are two distinct communication situations: one-to-one and in a group.

One-to-one communication

In one-to-one communication it is essential that each person understands that the other has the *right* to their own opinion and the *right* to express that opinion providing always that they remember that it is only an opinion. Since both parties can and should express their opinion on a matter, it follows that each must also *listen actively* to the other's opinion. It is only by expressing your view on a subject and listening carefully to the other person's view that you will both fully understand the situation – as perceived by the two of you.

To make this sort of communication work, it is necessary to use a multi-part approach, shown here as an Interpersonal Communication Model.

INTERPERSONAL COMMUNICATION MODEL

■   The first person expresses their opinion on the subject

■   The second person expresses their opinion *on the subject* (and not on the other's opinion)

■   They both accept the areas of agreement and identify the areas of disagreement

■   Both people focus on and discuss the areas of disagreement in order to resolve the differences, if possible – this may require adopting a different position

■   An agreement is reached on the subject – either both accept the same position or the differences are recognised and acknowledged

If this model is used for all one-to-one business communications, then the team will communicate effectively and can focus on the real issues rather than defending their opinions.

Group discussion

Most groups find effective group discussion extremely difficult and meetings seem to decline into a series of entrenched positions with attacks being made on anyone not agreeing with the current speaker. These meetings also tend to have just a few people talking while the rest of the group sit silently. Resolution of the differences tends not to

RULES FOR GROUP DISCUSSION

- Select a Chairperson – this would normally be the team leader, but if the team leader is central to the discussion then someone else should take the role

- Appoint a Recorder – this person is to keep notes of what each person says and to record the result of the discussion. It is best if the Recorder is not a participant in the discussion but it is possible that the Chairperson can fulfil this role as well

- The Chairperson should ask all participants to give their opinion on the subject; while doing so, they may not criticise or attack another person's position

- When *everyone* in the group has expressed their opinion, the Chairperson outlines the area of agreement and identifies the differences of opinion. (In most meetings, there tend to be few areas of disagreement and these are usually limited to just one or two people.)

- The discussion should now focus only on the areas of disagreement and the objective must be to resolve the difference. The Chairperson should call on those who expressed the opposing views and then ask for other contributions

- The result of the discussion should be recorded and agreed happen and agreement on a subject eludes the participants. The outcome is often that the team leader makes an arbitrary decision and everyone has to accept it. The meeting breaks up with everyone suffering a certain amount of frustration and the time having been wasted.

This scenario occurs because the group has failed to establish the rules for group discussion. If a sensible approach is adopted (as in the box above), disagreements tend to be very limited and are frequently a matter of interpretation; differences are resolved quickly and everyone feels that the subject has been properly aired; and time has not been wasted in circular or pointless discussion.

Decision-making

A frequent failing within team decision-making is that the team does not fully utilise all their combined knowledge and skills and the decision is based more on the input of a very few people. To avoid this, a set of rules can be followed, as shown in the box below.

Action plans and delegation

Team performance can also be adversely affected by poor action planning and inefficient delegation. It is vital that the team leaders make sure that, once a decision has been reached (either in a group discussion or by the team leader acting alone), the action is delegated to the most appropriate person or group and that action plans for achieving the objective are prepared and agreed.

This does not have to be overly formal providing that the team leader is satisfied that the person responsible for the action has the ability and knows how to carry it out.

Enhancing team performance

Team communication and group decision-making can be taught, but it is important that you teach both the team

211

RULES FOR GROUP DECISION-MAKING

- Select a Chairperson – this *must* be the team leader for the project

- Appoint a Recorder – this person is to keep notes of what each person says and to record the result of the discussion

- The Chairperson must ask all participants to give their opinion on the subject; while doing so, they may not criticise or attack another person's position

- When *everyone* in the group has expressed their opinion, it is likely that some *fundamental* disagreements exist

- The discussion must focus on resolving these disagreements. The Chairperson must call on *everyone* to contribute so as to maximise the input of knowledge, experience and skill

- A decision that presents the lowest risk to the objectives of the team has to be reached

- The decision and actions should be recorded

leader and the team *at the same time*. One approach is to set up a team training session during which they undertake an exercise in group decision-making. This is best done by using one of the many 'survival' exercises on the market – these exercises are paper-based and allow the participants to undertake the process using a situation in which they are highly unlikely to be experienced, such as being lost in the jungle or marooned on an island.

These exercises ask the individuals to make a series of decisions about actions and equipment. They then have to reach a group decision on the same things. If the process is good and the team communication effective, then the team decision will be better than that of any individual. If the process is not efficient then one or more individuals will score higher than the team, thus showing their input was not properly utilised.

These exercises can be combined with an analysis of the team communication skills that is designed to show the importance of the communication process when trying to reach a group decision. This will help the individuals to understand the roles they have to play to ensure that group synergy occurs and that group communication is effective.

When it comes to action plans and delegation, it is best that the team leader is trained separately. Again, the use of exercises and role-plays will enable the skills to be learned and then the coaches can ensure they are being utilised effectively.

Goal-setting

It cannot be stressed too much that goal-setting is the key to performance and that managers must be well trained in the process of establishing team goals, setting goals with individual team members, monitoring performance and providing feedback. You will have already established the necessary training and coaching for the managers but in almost all companies there is an area outside managers' control in which performance and effectiveness in goal-setting must be improved – the cascading of corporate goals down to individual level.

Corporate goals need interpretation

The corporate goals, almost always set in financial terms (revenues, costs, profit margins, resources) and in terms of corporate performance (market share, penetration, quality criteria), are meaningful only to senior management and they need to be translated and interpreted so that the goals of the teams and individuals all add up to the corporate objectives. This is where problems occur. Senior management often believes that it can, rather arbitrarily, just hand down the goals to the division or function heads who, in turn, do exactly the same thing all the way down without consideration of what the goals really mean at the front line.

This approach frequently results in inappropriate goals being handed to front-line managers – goals for things that are outside their control. This has to be avoided – goals are only meaningful and motivational if they are realistic, challenging, *and apply to those things that are within the control of the person who has to achieve them*. There is little point in setting a sales manager a goal for 'profit' when the actual pricing and profit margins (the things that determine profitability) are outside the manager's control. The sales manager must be set *sales volumes* as these are determined by sales activity which is in their control.

Goals must be realistic and achievable

Another issue is the size and scope of the goals. While it is totally appropriate for senior management to have huge and very challenging objectives, the further down the organisation you go the more important it is that the goals are realistic and achievable. At front-line levels, the individuals and the teams *must achieve their goals* and that means that they must be within reach. Failure to hit the target at this level is highly demotivational and likely to result in a decline in morale and performance.

It is a significant failure in leadership if a senior manager allows unrealistic or unachievable goals to be cascaded. To avoid this, you should establish a goal-setting process to ensure that the goals that come down are realistic. Once this has been done you will be able to address the all-too-common attitude that the goals don't count. Managers must be made aware that achieving their goals is a direct responsibility of their job and that a failure to do so is a failure to deliver that responsibility and it will count against them when the time comes to appraise performance.

Annual appraisals

Performance is appraised in two ways: there is the ongoing monitoring and feedback which leads to performance being appraised all the time, and there is the annual appraisal during which each person in the company is assessed as to whether they have achieved everything they are supposed to achieve, and delivered the level of performance required of them by the job description. This is also the time to determine what developmental needs they have and what career moves are possible.

If reviews are being done regularly and properly, by the time the annual appraisal comes round there should be no surprises in terms of performance against goals. The real objective of the process should be to act as a check that the Minimum Performance Standards (MPS) for each part of the job have been delivered consistently and to an acceptable standard and to assess the developmental needs of the individual. To achieve this requires input from a variety of sources and it should be the direct responsibility of *the individual concerned* to obtain all the information; it should not be left to the person's manager.

This is a radical shift in thinking for most human resource departments. Historically, annual appraisals are a personnel requirement operated by managers and team leaders; unfortunately, this has meant that it has been done badly in some circumstances and not done at all in many (perhaps most) cases. Companies seem to find it extraordinarily difficult to get managers to carry out annual appraisals and to do them on time – mainly because of the extra work involved over a short period. By transferring the responsibility to the individual concerned, you can relieve the pressure on the manager and encourage the individuals to take direct responsibility for their own development.

All-round appraisal

To make this a reality requires you to establish an effective appraisal system that is designed to collect the information required. Since the primary objectives are to check delivery of the job description and identify the developmental needs, you will need to collect information from the individual, their manager, their mentor, their colleagues and their subordinates if applicable. Such a process will need to protect the anonymity of their colleagues and subordinates so that genuine feedback is given.

This approach is sometimes called 360-degree Appraisal – but some confusion is associated with this: true 360-degree Appraisal would also involve those people outside the immediate team who come into contact with the individual regularly – for example, you would need feedback from customers or clients when assessing anyone in a customer-interface role. In the circumstances, it may be better to call the approach the 'All-Round Appraisal' and to limit it to the team concerned.

Data collection

The simplest process would be to establish a comprehensive questionnaire covering all the job responsibilities. The questions would be phrased so that the respondent can grade their answer; for example:

My goals are correctly set on a regular basis   5 4 3 2 1 0
Performance feedback is easily available to me   5 4 3 2 1 0
My performance is reviewed before new goals are set 5 4 3 2 1 0

The numerical grade could be either: 5 = always, 4 = usually, 3 = occasionally, 2 = hardly ever, 1 = never, 0 = not applicable; or the questions could be phrased so that the grading ranges from 5 = strongly agree to 1 = strongly disagree.

Working with the results

Each person involved would complete a questionnaire anonymously except for the manager, the individual and the mentor. The data would then be correlated to see where the gaps are. For example, if the individual claims to set goals correctly and regularly, provide feedback, and review performance before setting goals, but the subordinates disagree, then it is clear that here is an area that needs to be reviewed for further development.

If the questionnaire is properly constructed, then the individual will be able to see where they are falling short of the standards expected. They will also be able to undertake the appraisal interview with their manager properly prepared – after all, the manager will also have seen a copy of the results and will have the same information.

This approach allows the individual and their manager to focus on what really matters – the gaps in performance against MPS and the resulting developmental needs. It eliminates false perceptions such as can arise when the individual is very good at managing the relationship with their boss but not so good at managing their team; it also focuses attention on facts and not personalities.

Using the results

Once the appraisal has been completed, the manager and the individual can put together the development action plan covering the training and coaching that will be needed for the person to meet their MPS or to be ready to take on additional responsibilities. The results will also show whether the person meets the criteria for an increase in salary or benefits. In both cases, the results and the action plans will be used by the human resource director to plan the following year's training and coaching programme and the allocation of people throughout the company.

Recognition and reward

People often work harder for recognition than they do for reward. This is a fact that many companies do not fully understand but it is well documented and supported by research carried out around the world. Financial reward – payment over and above base salary – has little impact unless the bonus is a very significant percentage above salary. A bonus of £1,500 is a significant percentage (10%) if the base salary is £15,000 but is insignificant (5%) if the salary is £30,000. What is worse, the bonus will attract tax at the highest rate the individual pays and a £1,500 bonus is likely to attract between 25% and 40% tax – so the person will only receive between £900 and £1,125 which reduces the value of the reward very considerably.

On the other hand, non-financial recognition is highly prized and receiving an additional allocation of vacation, a better office, a bigger company car, or a different functional title can have a major impact on motivation and performance. Additionally, you should remember that junior employees also value such recognition as having a meeting with the CEO or MD, attending a conference, or representing the company at an outside event. A boost to motivation can also be given through the public recognition of performance acknowledged at a team meeting.

Raising someone's pay grade or corporate title should only come as a result of an annual appraisal and the decision of the company to increase the responsibilities of the individual. It is wise to keep in mind the fact that any particular job has an associated 'value' in terms of pay and conditions and, unless you have allocated a pay range, an increase in pay or conditions must be associated with a change in responsibilities. And, of course, the person will require a new job description to reflect the new responsibilities associated with the title or pay grade.

Recognising and rewarding superior performance is vital if motivation is to be maintained and it must always be given in public. The key is that the performance must be 'superior' – rewarding someone for hitting their MPS is damaging to the credibility of the process since the MPS is the very minimum that the person has to deliver to keep their job: delivering the MPS merely means that they have earned their salary. On the other hand, if the person also achieves performance-enhancing goals that are well above the MPS, they should be recognised. If they surpass the goals by 10% or more then they should receive additional recognition and a reward. We do not pay people to achieve more than their MPS and if they deliver *added value* they should be paid more.

But high achievers, people who surpass challenging goals, are not necessarily suitable for promotion: performance should be rewarded but promotion must be earned by demonstrating the ability to take on higher level responsibilities.

Promotions

The reasons for promoting anyone must be exactly the same reasons as for recruiting someone – you have a job that needs to be done, a job description exists for the role, and the person being promoted is the best candidate for the position. To promote for any other reason is to risk having the wrong person in the job.

There is always a temptation to assume that because

someone has done well in their current role they will be equally able to perform in a more senior role involving increased and different responsibilities. This is a dangerous assumption to make and it can lead to a situation in which a person ends up in a position that he is not competent to fill – the very situation identified by Lawrence Peter in his famous book *The Peter Principle*. When a person ends up in such a position they tend to focus on the work of their subordinates, to prefer to do the work of the role they have just left, and to avoid the responsibilities of their current job.

People who have done well in their current role should be rewarded, certainly, but they should only be promoted if there is a real job for them to do and they have the competencies and skills to meet the responsibilities and to deliver the MPS of the new job. For this reason, it is vital that you establish a recognition and reward system that does not rely on promotions.

Identifying candidates for promotion

Given the cost of recruitment, all companies need to develop their people so that a ready supply of future supervisors and managers is available internally. These people are identified from their annual appraisals as much as by their managers and you will need to put in place a review process so that you can identify and watch potential 'high flyers' – people capable of being developed to take on more senior roles.

Having found a selection of 'high flyers', you will need to undertake a careful analysis of the skills and attributes they have and determine those that they lack. With these in mind, you can set up special training sessions or send the people on selected training courses so that they round out and develop the missing skills. To exercise the new skills requires careful planning but it should be possible to allocate these people to a small role at a higher level so that you can assess how well the skills have been learned.

This process is not the same as promoting the person – if they fail to deliver then they will have the new responsibilities taken away and will revert to their original role.

How to promote

Many companies allow their staff to assume greater responsibility without going through a proper selection process – this is an error. You should insist that everyone seeking promotion, or identified for a higher position, must go through a full set of recruitment interviews and only if they turn out to be the right person for the job should they be given the new role. Promotion must never be a foregone conclusion and it must certainly not be based on seniority.

The process for promotion is, therefore, exactly the same as for recruitment, as described in Part One.

When to promote

There are two possibilities: to promote whenever a position needs filling, or to promote as part of a business cycle. Obviously, promoting when a position needs filling is the ideal but there are many companies that use the second possibility, as they see promotion as following the annual appraisal. The danger here is that promotion becomes associated with performance and thus a recognition or reward. Although this may not be the case, perceptions are important and it may be wise to address this.

There are very good reasons for promotions to be announced as part of a business cycle and the most powerful is when *all* promotions are announced together. This presupposes that you have an active career management process in place in which people are moved round (and up) as part of a continuous development process. This is a very practical approach but it does require a reasonably large company to make it work. In smaller companies there are just not enough jobs available to make this practical.

Final thoughts

The people who work for your company are the singularly most complex and costly resource that you have. They contract to work diligently and you pay them accordingly. But they walk out of your premises each night and you have no certainty that they will walk back in the following day and you must not take them for granted. You must not expect them to add value over and beyond what they have contracted for, nor can you allow them to produce less. It behoves you to plan the utilisation of your people for the benefit of the company but this does not mean you can adopt a cavalier approach: the 'hire-and-fire' school of managing people is counter-productive and demonstrates a lack of strategic planning; the arbitrary 'bums-on-seats' approach to recruitment leads to the wrong people being in the wrong job; and failing to develop your people leads to stagnation and the inability to make your company grow.

If you are going to recruit and develop top-quality people, you must plan their work, set the standards required, and ensure they deliver the performance they have agreed to. Every member of your staff is capable of delivering outstanding performance and it is your responsibility to ensure that the conditions in your company are such that outstanding performance is the norm.

Nothing must be left to chance – your objective must be to have the right people, with the right skills, managed and led in the right way.

The strategic management of human resources is the most important leadership function that senior managers can deliver. The development of top-quality people is part of this, and by implementing the ideas and techniques outlined in this book, you can ensure that your company achieves success.

Statutory public holidays

Statutory public holidays generally relate to religious festivals, cultural events or traditional workers' holidays. In some countries, if the public holiday falls on a weekend then an additional holiday of one working day is given in its place. In this way, most of the public holidays means that a working day is 'lost'.

Austria	**15 days**
Belgium	**14 days**
Canada	**12 days**
Denmark	**12 days**
Finland	**14 days**
France	**13 days**
Germany	**15 days**
Greece	**14 days**
Holland	**11 days**
Ireland	**10 days**
Italy	**12 days**
Japan	**14 days**
Luxembourg	**12 days**
Norway	**13 days**
Portugal	**14 days**
Spain	**15 days**
Sweden	**13 days**
Switzerland	**13 days**
United Kingdom	**9 days**
United States of America	**11 days**

Index

of senior management team 196–204
staff commitment, encouraging 150,
151
timeframe 168–9, 171–3
training, relationship with 157,
172–3
who is mentored 155–7, 170–1
minimum performance standards
(MPS) 78
annual appraisals 207, 215–18
coaching 113, 142
compensation, relationship with
16–17
in job description 10, 16–17
probationary period 74, 77
setting 17
skills, correct use of 112
mission statement 71
mobility 35
monitoring
coaching follow-up 112
managerial resistance to 143–7
mentoring programme 177–8
new staff 75–8
mortgage guarantees 26
motivation
developing soft skills 187–8
and goals 214
orientation training 87–8
and performance-enhancing goals 81
team leader's role 106

new staff
checklist 68–9
first impressions, importance 66
interviewing see interviewing
recruitment candidates
management responsibilities 66–73
orientation seminar 71, 87–8
pre-start activities 66–7
probationary period see probationary
period
recruitment see recruitment
references, checking 66
regular monitoring 75–8
security processes 67
skills deficiencies 87
supervision 69–70
training see training
welcoming 67, 69

observation, and coaching 115, 117
orientation training 86, 87–8
seminar for new staff 71
as team-building device 88
overalls, provision 66

pensions 22, 23
probationary period, during 74
people-management
developing as skill 187–8, 193, 194
management, by 184, 187, 193, 194
mentor, by 157–8
performance
acknowledging 207, 218–19
annual appraisals 207, 215–18
appraisal by mentor 163
bonuses related to 22, 24–5
development see performance
development
goals see performance-enhancing
goals
mentoring see mentoring
monitoring, managerial resistance to
143–7
pay linked to 152
performance-management skills,
developing 187–8
performance-related problems 73
recognition and reward 207, 218–19
performance development
coaching 113–16, 140–3
training 90
performance-enhancing goals (PEGs)
16, 78–80
agreeing 79, 80
feedback 80–1
measurable 80
psychological aspect 78
purpose 81
quality type 78–9
realistic 80
setting 79
specific 80
structure 78
timed 80
performance management 207
presentation skills 17
probationary period
appraisal form 76–7
completion 77–8, 79–80
duration 75
generally 73–4
holiday entitlement 74
job title 74–5
pension schemes 74
performance standards 74, 77
regular monitoring 75–8
unfair dismissal 75
productivity
and technology 7–8
training investment return,
measuring 101–2